ASSESSING THE NEEDS OF BILINGUAL PUPILS

LIVING IN TWO LANGUAGES

DERYN HALL

David Fulton Publishers

London

David Fulton Publishers Ltd
2 Barbon Close, London WC1N 3IX

First published in Great Britain by
David Fulton Publishers Ltd 1995
Reprinted 1995, 1996

British Library Cataloguing in Publication Data
A catalogue record for this book is available from the British Library.

ISBN 1-85346-332-9

Printed in Great Britain by Bell and Bain Ltd, Glasgow

Contents

Acknowledgements

This book was produced as part of my work for the London Borough of Tower Hamlets in helping schools with the identification and assessment of bilingual pupils causing learning concern. I have been fortunate to work alongside colleagues from the Language Support Service, the Educational Psychology Service and the Support for Learning Service as well as many teachers from mainstream primary and secondary schools who have provided a sounding board for the ideas included here.

I am particularly indebted to John Hutchings, Principal Educational Psychologist, Tower Hamlets for pointing me in the right direction and for alerting me to some of the pioneering work done in this field via articles in the Information Exchange for Educational Psychologists. These were edited and published by John from 1985 to 1989 in the days of the Inner London Education Authority.

Thanks also go to my colleagues in the Language Support central team, the local schools where I have worked and to the bilingual children of London's East End for providing me with a constant source of challenge, material and inspiration for this handbook.

Preface

This handbook is offered as a guide to all teachers working in multilingual and multicultural schools.

Together with some background information, it offers some practical ways of raising and considering the issues involved in the assessment of bilingual pupils whose learning is causing concern. Unfortunately there are no magic answers; no simple tests or instant solutions. However, I remain convinced that it is teachers and schools who have within their power the means which will lead to a greater awareness and more accurate assessment of the needs of these pupils.

There may be a wide variety of reasons why a bilingual child is not learning successfully at school and these will need to be fully considered before assumptions of learning difficulty are made

The Code of Practice (DFE 1994) now sets a clear expectation that the school will actively seek parents' (and older pupils' own) views where learning difficulties are registered. The expertise of language support staff, bilingual staff, community advice and interpreters/translators may also enhance early identification and assessment of SEN.

The main concern for teachers of bilingual pupils learning in a second language is how to separate temporary issues of language acquisition from longer term learning difficulties. It is in response to these voiced concerns that this handbook is offered.

1 Introduction

There has long been an unacknowledged relationship between bilingualism and special education as evidenced by the disproportionate numbers of immigrant and minority language children "deported" into special education classes ... in many countries.'
(Cummins 1984)

'Handicapping conditions do not respect ethnic, geographical, religious or any other boundaries imposed by man.'
(Miller 1984)

ACKNOWLEDGING OUR PLURALISTIC SOCIETY

Much educational literature is still produced without any reference to the fact that Britain is increasingly a multicultural and multilingual society.There is little excuse for this as it can no longer be seen as merely an issue for inner city schools. Linguistic diversity is now a norm in British classrooms. Most teachers across the country can expect to have some experience of pupils whose first language is other than English. Because, on the whole, schools continue to reflect the middle-class monocultural, monolingual values of a majority society, pupils' academic potential (or IQ) is still assessed in relation to these norms. Fortunately, larger numbers of immigrant and minority language pupils and a concern for educational equality of opportunity have caused educators to re-examine some of these assessment practices and to acknowledge that they may be inappropriate for increasing number of pupils.

Any assessment of bilingual pupils' learning progress needs to ascertain whether a pupil has a learning disability or is merely experiencing a temporary language barrier as a result of insufficient exposure to English. Unfortunately this assessment is no simple matter, and there is no single test which is also language and culture bias-free which can provide ready made answers. Rather, the issue begs a wide range of further questions. What is the nature of learning ability and disability? What are the principles of language acquisition? What is the relationship between first and second language skills? How long does it take to acquire English proficiency and what do we mean by that?

These questions and issues cause monolingual teachers (and educational psychologists) considerable anxiety when the educational progress of a bilingual child is giving concern. This handbook suggests that the information gained will only be as good as the questions asked, the information/evidence of learning gathered and the teaching provision/intervention made. These issues are further explored in Chapters 4, 5 and 6.

SEPARATING ISSUES OF 'LANGUAGE' FROM 'LEARNING'

Since litigation in the USA of the late 1960's and early1970's, educators have been at pains to spell out the necessity of distinguishing between second language barriers and learning difficulties which may account for an individual bilingual pupil's failure to make learning progress. A landmark case (Diana v. State Board of Education, California 1970) established rights to a non biased assessment for ethnic minority pupils. So that, in the 1981 Education Act which served to define special educational needs for England and Wales, the following clear statement appeared:

'A child is not to be taken as having a learning difficulty solely because the language (or form of language) in which he is, or will be, taught is different from a language (or form of language) which has at any time been spoken in his home'

It is important that the provision made for English as a Second Language is not confused with special educational needs remediation. It is a sad reflection of the 1990's that some teachers still equate a lack of English language skills with 'learning problems' and low intelligence.

Some pupils whose first language is not English will need support to extend their speaking and writing repertoires and to practise new words and phrases in a relevant context. They will need to acquire sufficient linguistic competence in order that their understanding of processes and concepts is fully developed. A recent OFSTED (Office for Standards in Education) paper (1994) describes some of the most effective lessons as those which "included the use of specially prepared materials to match the pupils' levels of English and educational experience, and tasks which enabled them to work purposefully with their peers and encouraged them to become increasingly independent of support."

Pupils with special educational needs, on the other hand, may require specific targeted support for their individual learning difficulty (this may also involve support for a specific disability or for emotional/ behavioural difficulty). The guidance issued in the 1994 Code of Practice suggests that such identified pupils should be formally registered on a SEN "stage of concern" by the school and their progress regularly monitored in consultation with parents and in partnership with other professionals. At school based stages 2 and 3 this will involve drawing up an Individual Education Plan (IEP see Chapter 6).

However, both groups of pupils require support in order to gain full access to the curriculum to which they have entitlement..To some extent, it could be argued that what is good practice for one group is also good practice for the other, as the necessary degree of curriculum differentiation, thought and planning evidenced in successful lessons would inevitably improve the learning of all pupils. One such example of integrated good practice is described in "a school with a multi-disciplinary team approach (SEN, home/school liaision and S11 staff) to meet the learning needs of individual pupils. Careful planning and systematic record keeping ensured that only one additional teacher participated in any one lesson but that all teachers worked to the agreed programme of support." (OFSTED 1994)

However, distinction must be clearly made between the individual learning needs of bilingual pupils and pupils with SEN and different appropriate provision needs to be offered. Schools must ensure that lack of English proficiency is not assumed to indicate special educational needs or learning difficulties.

Not withstanding, a percentage of bilingual pupils is likely to experience special educational needs at some point of their school life and there is no hard evidence to suggest that this is either more or less than we might expect to find in the monolingual population. As this is reckoned nationally to be plus or minus 20% of the school population, we can expect a proportionate and representative spread of bilingual pupils to be at each SEN stage at any given time. This is a fairly crude figure but is a simple measure which a school can use as an indicator of the understanding of the issues involved within their institution.

A LANGUAGE APPROACH TO THE CURRICULUM

It is now universally agreed that language in its broadest sense of 'communicative competence' is central to the learning process in the acquisition of a second language.It was previously believed that bilingual pupils learning English needed different teaching methods and materials which were somehow separate from those relevant or appropriate to other pupils. Linguists and educationalists have recognised that the teaching methodologies developed as a response to mixed ability classes are also those which are relevant and appropriate for bilingual learners. The slow recognition of the growing linguistic diversity of mainstream classrooms has reinforced the need to find inclusive teaching methods and materials.

It has also become clear that exclusive methodologies could threaten equality of opportunity and be seen as racially divisive. As a direct result of the findings of Swann (DES 1985) and the Calderdale investigation (CRE 1986), separate off-site withdrawal units for pupils new to English were deemed as clearly discriminatory on social, linguistic and educational grounds. It is now standard practice in this country to try to support pupils learning English as a second language within the mainstream classroom as part of normal lessons. Furthermore there is considerable interest from some other European countries who are looking at the best of this inclusive practice in Britain as a model of how to educate their own recent refugee or immigrant populations.

Encouraging skills and versatility in speaking and listening is vital in developing understanding of ideas and experiences. The process of thinking out loud, formulating thought and talking through ideas are an essential part of the learning process. Pupils who engage orally in the language of a subject with their peers are more likely to understand and internalise the related concepts. Language teachers working in partnership with mainstream curriculum colleagues to plan collaborative group activities can help to provide learning materials in which contextual clues ensure fuller access to tasks for all pupils. (Many practising teachers using this methodology 'swap' their teaching materials through membership of the

Collaborative Learning Project; see Useful Addresses at end of handbook) This allows bilingual pupils, as well as those with learning difficulties, more chance of working on their understanding at an appropriate cognitive level of challenge than materials which are reliant on decoding skills alone. Typical exchanges during oral collaborative tasks might include practising language structures such as questioning, reflecting, suggesting, prediction and forming hypotheses.

For some bilingual pupils the opportunity to use their first/home language to support learning and understanding in the classroom will provide a way of enhancing the conceptualisation of complex ideas and confirm language and meaning. Bilingual pupils, particularly those from minority immigrant or refugee groups, need support to gain good academic qualifications without which their employment prospects will be drastically reduced. This should not be at the expense of their first language skills however, as their facility and literacy in dual languages is also a marketable commodity.

2 Bilingual Pupils

A WORKING DEFINITION

There have been many attempts to define bilingualism during the past fifty years and these range from earlier narrow definitions to the broader ones of Skutnabb-Kangas [1981]. The one used in this book and from which it takes its subtitle, is the working definition adopted by the London Borough of Tower Hamlets [1992]

Bilingual: *In England the term is currently used to refer to pupils who live in two languages, who have access to, or need to use, two or more languages at home and at school. It does not mean that they have fluency in both languages or that they are competent and literate in both languages.*

DIFFERENT GROUPS OF BILINGUAL CHILDREN

Teachers cannot assume that all bilingual children they may come across in schools are one homogenous group. There are likely to be differing pressures depending on the context in which the pupils need to acquire the new language and these will determine the pupils' investment in learning. Bilingual pupils fall roughly into the following categories:

ELITE BILINGUALS:

These are the children of those families who travel abroad from choice, usually for business, academic or diplomatic reasons. They are often children of upper/middle class professionals whose first language is in no way threatened and which is maintained at home and by visits home. For these children bilingualism even if they do not achieve full fluency in their second language.

LINGUISTIC MAJORITIES:

This group of pupils are those from a large group where they are learning a second language either because the schools offer a more prestigious minority /or world language e.g. English in Hong Kong, or offer an immersion programme such as French immersion in Canada.

BILINGUAL FAMILIES:

Some children will come from homes where a different language is spoken by one parent. If this is a minority language then there is no external pressure to become bilingual even though there may well be family, cultural or religious pressure e,g, from grandparents.

LINGUISTIC MINORITIES:

This is likely to be the group of most concern to teachers. Whether they are from refugee or other immigrant families the home language is likely to have a low status or value in the new society. Children from these families will be subjected to strong pressure to learn the language of the majority community and will need to become competent in speaking, reading and writing for economic survival. They are also likely to have pressure from their families to take advantage of better educational opportunities but also strong pressure to retain their first language and culture. For the children from the Bangladeshi community in the East End of London this often means learning standard Bengali, and mosque Arabic as well as learning English at school and retaining the spoken home language of Sylheti.

WHAT THE RESEARCH TELLS US

The following list is a summary of the most important points to emerge from the extensive research into the acquisition of second language. (Cummins 1984; Dulay, Burt & Krashen 1982; Desforges & Kerr 1984; Skutnabb-Kangas 1984) *See photocopiable sheet on page 76.* They are well substantiated and should be adopted by teachers as basic premises.

- Children take up to two years to develop 'basic interpersonal communication skills' (playground/street survival language) BUT it takes from five to seven years to acquire the full range of literacy skills ('cognitive academic language proficiency') needed to cope with the literacy demands of GCSE.

- A silent (receptive) period is natural in the learning of a second language and not a sign of learning difficulties in the first/early stages.

- There are developmental factors common to both native and second language acquisition. Pupils learn roughly the same regardless of their first language background.

- Teachers /schools should have basic information available about the language backgrounds of bilingual pupils. (see Chapter 4)

- There should be an awareness by all that a focus on mother tongue is a valuable channel to support learning and NOT a hindrance. Teachers should not advocate the use of English only, either at school or at home.

- Parents should be encouraged to share language and literacy in speaking and listening as well as in reading and writing. This can be as valuable in first/home language as in English.

- Bilingualism can be educationally enriching and has a positive effect on intellectual performance.

- Bilingualism should be valued as a special achievement.

- Where there are academic difficulties, teachers should first critically examine the teaching they are offering in terms of motivation and the language used.

GOOD PRACTICE IN TEACHING BILINGUAL PUPILS

There is a wide consensus in this country as to what constitutes good practice in the teaching of bilingual children in the mainstream classroom. The view now is that the education of bilingual pupils is the responsibility of all teachers and not simply that of ESL or bilingual support staff where these are available. The methodologies of partnership teaching, active teaching and learning, collaborative and group work, and the role of oracy in classrooms all contribute to a body of knowledge about good practice which have a particular relevance for bilingual pupils.(See the practical ideas for language work in primary schools in Shell 1992 and Buxton 1994)

PARTNERSHIP TEACHING

One of the arguments for the promotion of partnership teaching [Bourne and McPake 1991], for example, is that with dwindling resources and Section 11 funding cuts, the emphasis must be on changing practice to take account of the diversity of both language and learning needs within the classroom. The implications of lack of additional support for bilingual pupils are that the curriculum offered must be accessible and relevant to all pupils' needs and teachers should evaluate their practice in meeting these needs accordingly.

Partnership teaching as described in Bourne & McPake (1991) is a broader model than that of one class or subject teacher working together with one language support teacher inside a classroom. It requires a committment from the senior management of the school to a model of shared planning and the expertise of pairs or groups of teachers and other partners working together to access curriculum both inside and outside the classroom. The organisation of the classroom to enable pupils to work in groups and the benefit of this for bilingual pupils cannot be emphasised enough.

ORACY: THE ROLE OF TALK IN CLASSROOMS

Talk is a vital key to language acquisition and the active learning strategies encouraged by the National Oracy Project [1987-1993] demonstrated the benefit of talk in the learning process. Encouraging skills and versatility in speaking and listening is vital in developing understanding of ideas and experiences. Pupils are expected to produce written outcomes as evidence of learning in our examination systems. Yet speech is the primary instrument of thought and argument. Expressive narrative, story telling and writing are important links in learning to the production of transactional formal prose. Douglas Barnes [1992] aptly describes the role of talk in classrooms as a way of "working on understanding". It is no accident that OFSTED inspectors are asked to comment on oracy, equated with literacy and numeracy, across the curriculum. Pupils encouraged to express themselves orally are also ultimately more likely to have a voice in democratic society.

USE OF MOTHER TONGUE IN CLASSROOMs

For bilingual pupils, the opportunity to use first language at school is a way of confirming language and meaning to support learning. Many bilingual pupils come from cultures with a strong oral tradition. For example, the Somali language had no written form until 1972 and all religious, academic and cultural learning was handed down orally. These oral literacy traditions which are vital to the well being of a culture, rely on very advanced skills of memory speaking and listening and we should capitalise on these and acknowledge that some will need fostering and reviving.

Pupils must be encouraged to use their first languages in the classroom but will be more prepared to support their learning and understanding in this way if their community language is given a high status at school. For this reason pupils' home languages and experiences must be not only valued and recognised in school but developed and utilised. Parents also frequently need help and reassurance to recognise the vital role that sustaining and developing oracy and literacy in the home language can play in learning. Research proves that facility in first language is a help rather than a hindrance to learning in a second language. Sadly, children whose own first language is not well established by school age are statistically likely to be at a severe disadvantage in acquiring a second language as the underlying conceptual and linguistic proficiency will not be sufficiently developed to aid transfer. (Cummins 1984)

ACTIVE AND COLLABORATIVE LEARNING IN SMALL GROUPS

Pupils working cooperatively on tasks in groups share skills and support each other. This method of delivering curriculum emphasises and actively encourages oral work which helps to formulate and expand ideas. During the problem solving process pupils are using skills of negotiating, prioritising, investigating, drafting, sequencing and matching.

Using active learning strategies in the classroom frees teachers from the traditional role of instructor for some of the time. This enables them to spend more time with small groups or special needs pupils needing additional support as the class is organised to work on tasks in groups. It also engenders a sense of personal involvement, self esteem and ownership among pupils. These are all important factors in empowering them to take responsibility for their own learning. The talk engendered by the group process maximises opportunities for bilingual pupils to order, classify and transform information and to experience, test, shape and interpret meaning. How groups are organised can be a vital element in their success. Pupils new to English need to be grouped with supportive peers, particularly if there is a shared first language. However it is not good practice to group all mother tongue speakers together as groups need to include good pupil models of English. Many proven models of group organisation, balance and change are provided by Reid et al [1989]

THE IDENTIFICATION AND ASSESSMENT OF PUPILS CAUSING CONCERN

WHAT IS IT?

The Home Office clearly requested that Section 11 funded project teachers should monitor targeted bilingual students using language levels or stages. Many local education authorities (LEAs) based their models on the work of Hilary Hester (Barrs et al 1990). Using variations of her published Language Stages (which are descriptions of language behaviour in its broadest communicative sense), Section

11 teachers have assessed and plotted the progress of bilingual pupils. Interpreting these has led to much local discussion and the need for moderation in many LEAs. A consensus as to what evidence at each stage is looked for across the four language skills of listening, speaking, reading and writing has been developed in many parts of the country.(see Chapter 5)

Teachers and departments who have been supporting bilingual learners in schools in the past few years have built up considerably knowledge and expertise in normative (related to their school population and locality) expected rates and patterns of progress in the acquisition of English. Often they have considerable understanding of patterns of typical errors made by particular linguistic groups which relate to the differences and structures in the first language. (see Chapter 5)

Where there is informed concern about lack of progress in learning across time, the question must be raised as to whether the pupil should be registered under the Code of Practice [Education Act 1993] as having special educational needs.

Although some bilingual pupils are likely to experience special educational needs in much the same way as the indigenous population, these pupils need to be clearly distinguished from those in the early stages of acquiring English. (see Chapter 7)

WHY SHOULD WE DO IT?

Teachers are required to assess pupils' learning progress as part of the normal cycle of planning, teaching and assessing. If second language acquisition is confused with cognitive learning difficulties; or cultural adjustment with social adjustment and behaviour difficulties; we risk falling into the trap of falsely labelling and inappropriately educating young people who will either under achieve or suffer entrenched difficulties as a result of being falsely identified. In the past such mistakes were made and we need to work with greater sensitivity and increased awareness in the light of the greater knowledge and experience available to us.

There may be many reasons why a bilingual pupil is not learning successfully at school and all of these possible causes these must be considered before a child is 'registered' as having special educational needs.

HOW TO DO IT?

At the end of Chapter 3 a model or 'map' for the process of identifying and assessing bilingual pupils causing concern is introduced. By following subsequent chapters you will have a range of practical ideas which you can copy or adapt for use in your school

3 The Identification and Assessment of Bilingual Pupils causing concern.

'Second language learners who perform poorly in the school setting because of limited familiarity with English and/or cultural differences need to be distinguished from children who demonstrate communicative disorders and/or abnormalities that require special education intervention.'

[Mattes and Omark 1984]

THE ISSUES INVOLVED

It is vital that teachers distinguish between issues of lack of English language acquisition and those of learning where there is concern about a child's educational progress. The collection of information which may provide evidence which could inform such decisions is only likely to be as good as the questions asked. In fact many educational psychologists would claim that decisions cannot be made until such crucial basic information is collected. [Robson 1993] However, there is often a wealth of information available, held by different people or stored in different files around the school, which, if put together, would build a useful picture of the child. Once questions have been asked and evidence collected together then more accurate decisions as to the nature of appropriate support can be provided by the school.

Anna Wright (1991]) puts the dilemma facing professionals in assessing a bilingual child with reported learning difficulties very clearly. She claims that this process involves avoiding two errors:

- **FALSE POSITIVE**
  the error of diagnosing a learning difficulty where none is present, therefore labelling the child and possibly changing the mode of instruction or environment to one that is not suitable, for example, placing a child in a special school where the language environment may be less rich.

- **FALSE NEGATIVE**
  the error of failing to diagnose a learning difficulty and thus not giving the child appropriate help at an early stage, allowing subsequent difficulties to become more entrenched and harder to manage.

A HISTORICAL PERSPECTIVE

This neatly reflects the historical pattern of referral of bilingual children to special schools and units in this country. As early as the 1970's representatives of

15

Britain's minority communities expressed concern as to the over - representation of black and bilingual children in segregated provision. Coard (1971), Tomlinson (1981) and the Commission for Racial Equality (1986) have all drawn attention to the fact that pupils whose home language was not 'standard English' were discriminated against in their allocation to separate or special educational provision. *[false positive]*

In the 1980's, due to challenges to the racist assumptions which designated many bilingual children as having special educational needs in terms of their learning, there was an under referral of these pupils to specialist provision. At the same time there was an increasing awareness of the linguistic and cultural bias of many of the standardised tests, both here and in the U.S.A.. Unfortunately some bilingual children with extensive learning needs and sometimes with considerable sensory loss were therefore left for years before proper referral and assessment on the assumption that as they were bilingual they just needed ' more time'.
[false negative]

Hopefully with a better understanding of the need for language support for targeted pupils within the mainstream classroom and of the need to continually assess levels and rate of second language acquisition and learning across the curriculum, this situation is being rectified in the 1990's.

As stated in Chapter 1 there is no reason to suppose that any more or any less percentage of any one population is likely to experience special educational need as defined in the 1981 Education Act than any other. In fact, Circular 1/83 was at some pains to separate linguistic problems from learning difficulties and to specifically exclude those children whose sole difficulty was because the language of instruction was different from their home language. There is no doubt that proper identification and assessment of bilingual pupils has suffered from institutional and socially unjust practices in the past and that disproportionate numbers of black and bilingual pupils were either wrongly assessed or left with unidentified difficulties.

PROBLEMS OF STANDARD PSYCHOLOGICAL TESTS

There has been a realisation amongst many educational pyschologists (EPs) of the inappropriateness of most standardised tests which would otherwise be employed as part of the assessment of intellectual or learning difficulties of pupils experiencing difficulty at school. There is no test which serves to answer the question of whether or not a bilingual child has learning difficulties and EPs are very much reliant on the evidence presented by schools for the following reasons of inadequacy of the available tests:

CULTURAL BIAS

Standardised tests embody the values of Anglo-centric conformity by the assumption that everybody is a member of a homogenous cultural and statistical population. It has already been argued that we live in a pluralistic society where we are aware that many of the ethnic and language minorities have been exposed to very different learning experiences from middle class English children.

Since all learning occurs within a culture, tests can be considered to be culture loaded because test construction procedures are inevitably based on the culture of the dominant group. Even if items were specifically picked to reflect the unique learning experiences of individual minority groups they would be rejected in the item analysis because they would be 'difficult' for the majority group and thus would not correlate well with the total test; i.e. in psychometric terminology they are not 'good' items. It is not difficult to see how this construction biases tests against minority groups.

Even tests for young pre-school age children can make assumptions about the familiarity of play objects and experiences without the necessary awareness of cultural differences. The extent of any bias will depend on how different the socialisation/learning experiences of the child are from that of the majority in the representative sample.

LANGUAGE BIAS

Verbal tests are particularly prone to bias, moreover it is virtually impossible to design a verbal test appropriate for all bilingual children which is free of bias. No generally accepted alternatives to the use of English IQ tests exist which is why their use and interpretation is subject to such great caution by psychologists today. We know from the research literature that children from different cultural groups are exposed to different vocabulary. Even something so apparently simple as word association is fraught with difficulty as it depends on familiarity with the context and content of the problem.

TRANSLATION

Why then can tests not simply be translated from the English and administered by a native speaker? Apart from the arguments about cultural and linguistic bias, there are issues of differing syntax and structure which would render them unreliable and invalid tests across varying translations, languages and dialects.

POPULATIONS OF NORM REFERENCED TESTS

Some attempts have been made in parts of Britain to design and validate tests designed for one population of minority language children in a geographical area. e.g. Sandwell Bilingual Screening Assessment (Punjabi). This work on testing in minority languages has been pioneered by Speech and Language Services. However this is mainly to help in the difficult field of ascertaining specific language disorders in bilingual children rather than in the more general area of the testing of academic potential. Such tests are standardised and validated on local minority language populations so they are inevitably rendered unreliable for children from other language communities elsewhere.

There is a recent revival in tests which are being designed partly in response to interest by local education authorities in the concept of 'added value'. Because of the pressure from central government through standardised tests and published results, there is a need for greater accountability in order to prove the efficacy of teaching. As children start their formal schooling at such different stages of learning and experience, the use of baseline information is helpful as a starting point. It serves, at least, to say something about what part of their experiences children have learned from and to identify children's needs. This can give the teacher something to build upon at an early stage. It also serves to show how much progress is being made from a fixed point as a result of the teaching. For example, Birmingham's Baseline Assessment for all pupils in the Primary Phase has been running in over a hundred schools for the past year with reception class pupils assessed on their early skills in English and maths using criteria based on National Curriculum levels 1 and 2. In 1996 the LEA will be able to use this information to make a value added assessment when these pupils are tested on standard national tests (SATs). Among other things, this information will be useful to assess the advantages of nursery education, particularly for those children whose first language is not English.

INTRODUCING THE 'MAP' *(See photocopiable sheet on page 75)*

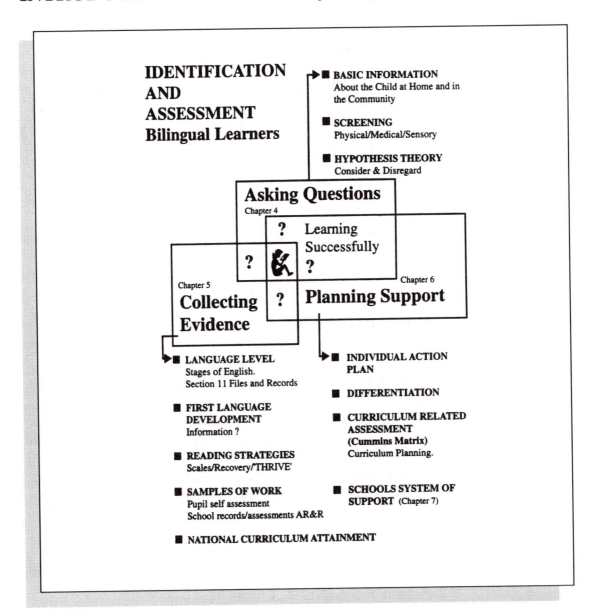

IDENTIFICATION AND ASSESSMENT Bilingual Learners

- **BASIC INFORMATION** About the Child at Home and in the Community
- **SCREENING** Physical/Medical/Sensory
- **HYPOTHESIS THEORY** Consider & Disregard

Asking Questions Chapter 4

? Learning Successfully ?

Collecting Evidence Chapter 5

Planning Support Chapter 6

- **LANGUAGE LEVEL** Stages of English. Section 11 Files and Records
- **FIRST LANGUAGE DEVELOPMENT** Information ?
- **READING STRATEGIES** Scales/Recovery/'THRIVE'
- **SAMPLES OF WORK** Pupil self assessment School records/assessments AR&R
- **NATIONAL CURRICULUM ATTAINMENT**

- **INDIVIDUAL ACTION PLAN**
- **DIFFERENTIATION**
- **CURRICULUM RELATED ASSESSMENT** (Cummins Matrix) Curriculum Planning.
- **SCHOOLS SYSTEM OF SUPPORT** (Chapter 7)

WHAT IS IT?

It ia a model or figure which begs the question as to whether a bilingual child is learning successfully at school. If there is any doubt about educational progress, or confusion as to whether the child may have special educational needs, the map offers you a route through which the various factors which may be causing a difficulty for a child learning in a second language can be explored. The following three chapters explore some of the existing theories and active ways in which teachers and schools can work towards a better informed decision by:

- asking questions
- collecting evidence
- planning support

This map puts together and builds on work and thinking from many different sources in the belief that greater awareness of issues makes for sound judgement.

WHY SHOULD WE DO IT?

Ann Robson who is a writer, researcher and practising senior educational psychologist clearly states that she is unable to reach a decision about the learning of a bilingual child until crucial information has been checked. This is her list:

- family/child history

- perceptions of parents/family; child; and teachers about learning progress and achievement

- physical health, medical information

- previous educational history and current education in school and community

- language knowledge and experience

- the context for learning in school and class

- evidence of a differentiated curriculum

- evidence of achievements to date, including samples of work

- evidence of other professionals involved

- community context and family status

Without a full examination of the many possible factors which may be causing difficulty, we risk not addressing the bilingual child's real needs at an early enough point. Conversely, we risk making wrong assumptions about a child's difficulty without first examining the adequacy of our own classroom practice. If good classroom practice is employed to include bilingual pupils in tasks set at an appropriate level of demand, with good visual access and opportunities to practice English language patterns in differing contexts, then pupils are likely to make good progress. It is out of concern for those pupils who don't that this map has been devised.

HOW TO DO IT?

Read the next three chapters which give some of the possible methodology which is often an inclusive part of normal good educational practice. You will raise your own level of awareness and in discussion with colleagues can use and adapt any of the material for your own purpose within school.

4 Asking Questions: assessing background information

In this chapter the premise is made that the answer to concerns about a child's lack of learning progress will only be as good as the questions asked. Subsequent chapters will look at other parts of the model in terms of collecting evidence and providing support.

BASIC INFORMATION ABOUT THE CHILD AT HOME AND IN THE COMMUNITY

WHAT IS IT?

- Basic information which will help every school to assess the learning needs of a bilingual child on admission.

The school needs to collect such basic information when a pupil is first admitted. In most schools and local education authorities specific standardised admission information is required as a matter of course. For bilingual children, schools need fuller information than the biographical details required for monolingual pupils as this will have implications for teaching and learning.

Additional details should be sought on:

LANGUAGES:

- What languages are used by individual members of the immediate family to the child?
- What languages are used by the child to them in return?
- Which languages can the child read? [is the child learning to read?]
- Which languages can the child write? [is the child learning to write?]

SOCIAL FACTORS:

- Information [and dates] about the number of terms previous schooling in the U.K.

- Information on previous schooling [and extent] abroad.

- Information on extended visits abroad, family separations [and dates].

- Details of names of both parents; names and ages of siblings.

- Details of family religion; festivals observed, dietary requirements.

- Family view of important illnesses or other medical factors seen as important.

COMMUNITY LINKS:

- Does the child attend any school / class / group in the community? How often?

- What is the name / address of the organisation?

- Who is the contact person for the group?

- What language is used / taught there?

WHY SHOULD WE DO IT?

- To provide a meeting point between parents and school.

- To provide a framework for discussion with parents.

- To emphasise the importance of working together to support the child's learning at school.

- To encourage the parents to continue to support first language development through storytelling, sharing books and reading in the home language.

- To collect a full picture about the languages in which the child is living and learning outside school

Good communication with parents should be established by the school as early as possible and the parents made to feel welcome.

Teachers need to be aware that:

- Parents will have experiences of their own schooling and these will not always be positive ones!

- In some cultures parents are not expected or encouraged to participate in the process of their child's education at school.

- Some parents may have had little formal schooling in their own countries or may be illiterate in the standard form of their language.

HOW DO WE ORGANISE IT?

The meeting should be held at school if possible, where the focus will be on helping the child learn successfully. Parents can be contacted by a Home/School Liaison teacher or by another adult worker at the school who speaks the home language.If absolutely necessary, most schools have access to translators who will be working within the community.

- Fill in an 'Information Form'. (*See Figure overpageand photocopiable sheet on page 77.*) The headings will act as an aide memoire in seeking full details

- Older pupils could simultaneously (or subsequently) be asked to fill in their own 'Languages Record'(*See Figure on page 24 and photocopiable sheet on page 76.*)

- A relaxed informal atmosphere is essential and the meeting should be regarded as a gathering of information and discussion rather than conducted as a formal questionnaire.

- Parents should be encouraged to add any information that they feel is relevant.

- They may wish to bring a friend or extended family member to provide support and/or to act as an interpreter.

- The school should be clear where the information will be stored and who will have access to it.

- Emphasise that the focus of the meeting is to help their child make the most of the learning opportunities at school

The Bilingual Pupil at Home and in the Community

Basic Family Details

Full Name .... D.O.B. ....

Name child is called at home .... Age Now ....

Name to be called at school (if different) ....

Arrival date in UK (if not British born) ....

Length of previous schooling abroad ....

Names of schools/LEAs in UK ....

Number of terms of UK schooling ....

Date of long extended absences from schooling ....

Place of birth .... Religion ....

Does child live with both parents as part of family unit? .... Festivals observed ....

If not who are carers? ....

Mothers name .... Dietary needs ....

Fathers name ....

(School correspondence should be addressed to ....

Most useful written language for family is ....

Names and ages of siblings ....

....

....

Languages

Languages spoken at home by pupil to   Mother .... Grandparents ....

                                            Father .... Siblings ....

Languages used by family members to child

Can child read/write languages other than English?   write .... read ....

Is child learning to read/write in languages other than English? ....

Community Links

Does child attend any school/class in community/ ....

Mother tongue class .... community school .... religious .... Mosque/classes ....

What languages are used taught there? ....

What is the name/address of organisation? ....

....

....

Who is contact person for group? ....

Is interpreter needed for teacher to communicate with parents ? ....

If so, who might this be? ....

Family view of important illnesses/or other medical factors seen as important ....

Is child right handed? left handed? .... Should child be using glasses hearing aid/other aids for learning? ....

Does child require any regular medication during school day ....

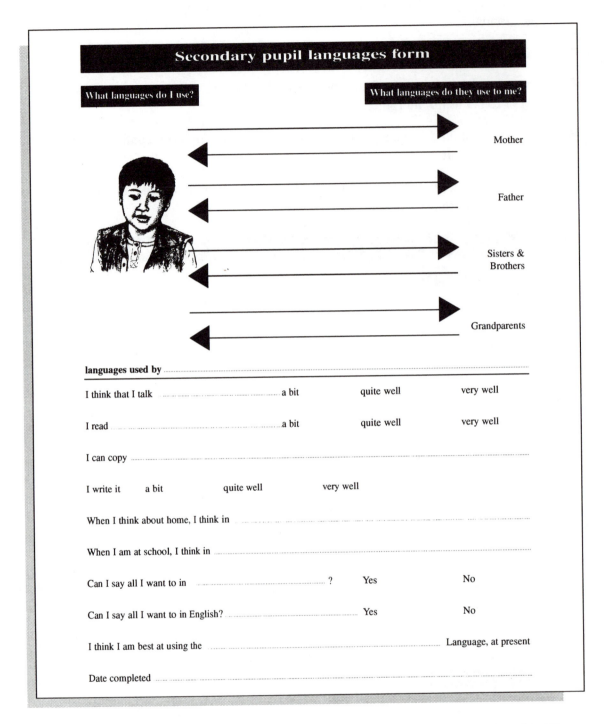

Secondary pupil languages form

What languages do I use? What languages do they use to me?

Mother

Father

Sisters & Brothers

Grandparents

languages used by ....

I think that I talk ....a bit   quite well   very well

I read ....a bit   quite well   very well

I can copy ....

I write it   a bit   quite well   very well

When I think about home, I think in ....

When I am at school, I think in ....

Can I say all I want to in ....?   Yes   No

Can I say all I want to in English? ....   Yes   No

I think I am best at using the .... Language, at present

Date completed ....

SCREENING FOR PHYSICAL / SENSORY PROBLEMS

WHAT ARE THEY?

It is easy to assume that all children entering school have had full health and developmental checks prior to admittance. In the U.K. this is normally the case. However, where there is cause for concern in learning in a bilingual pupil, one of the first questions to consider is whether the child's vision, hearing, general health and physical development is normal as they may not have had the usual screening.

- Does the child respond to her/his name being called?

- Does the child listen to and respond normally to other children and adults speaking her/his home language?

- Does the response from the child vary from day to day [good days and bad days]?

- Does the child seem particularly inattentive?

- Have you varied seating arrangements with a view to checking visibility of books, boards, easels used for class/group work and hearing?

- Does the child strain to see/have unusual difficulty copying from a model?

- Have you observed any unusual physical difficulties in PE lessons?

- Have you checked and shared your concern with others?

- Have you checked with parents?

WHY CHECK THIS?

Children who were born in or who are arriving from developing countries may have difficulties which have been missed or overlooked previously yet which are serious enough to cause learning problems. It is not always easy to distinguish these if the child is new to English and if there are emotional or adjustment difficulties. Teachers' experience of children will usually indicate when to feel concern. Although teachers will need to arrange checks through the school nurse and child health agencies, they are often in the position of providing clear evidence of the concern. It is vital that this concern is indicated to the appropriate professionals sooner rather than later. Trust your experience and the evidence! Bilingual children must not be left on the assumption that they "just need more time".

NB *Some conditions such as 'glue ear' are very common (one in every four children under five years). This causes intermittent hearing loss which can lead to serious problems in learning, particularly for a young child learning in a second language.*

HOW TO CHECK

- Check with colleagues and others who speak the child's home language.

- Discuss your concern with parents. Have they noticed? [by comparison to another child in the family?]

- Refer the child through the usual school channels to the school nurse. Ask them to check sight and hearing if there are no early health records.

HYPOTHESIS THEORY

WHAT IS IT?

This is a hypothesis testing approach which was developed by educational psychologists as a response to some of the difficulties faced in the assessment of bilingual children who may have learning difficulties. A five stage model developed by John Hutchins and the Educational Psychology Service in Tower Hamlets is included here to demonstrate how a hypothesis testing approach is helpful. It relies on the school collecting information and is a method of deciding what further information may be necessary to eliminate some of the possible reasons for, or causes of concern about a child's lack of progress. This has been further developed (Wright 91) as a list of possible reasons why a bilingual child may be failing at school. Each hypothesis comes with a list of suggested points to look at and consider. It also gives suggestions for contra-indications so that the hypothesis can be disregarded if there should be sufficient evidence to make it unlikely as a significant factor of a poor level of performance.

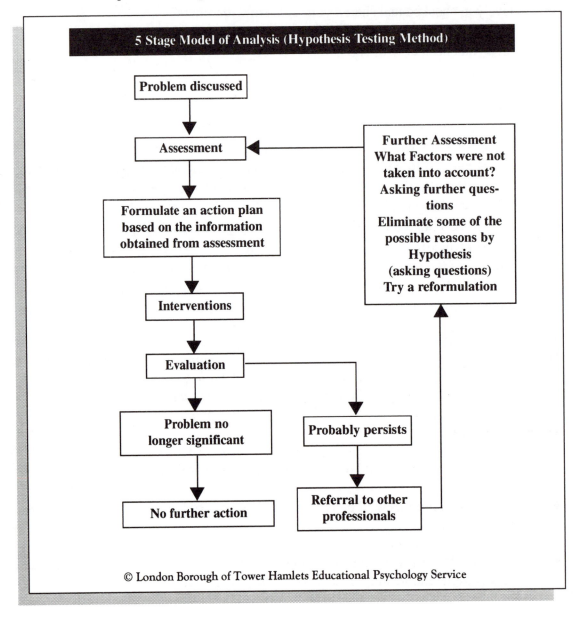

5 Stage Model of Analysis (Hypothesis Testing Method)

Problem discussed

↓

Assessment

↓

Formulate an action plan based on the information obtained from assessment

↓

Interventions

↓

Evaluation

→ Problem no longer significant → No further action

→ Probably persists → Referral to other professionals

Further Assessment
What Factors were not taken into account?
Asking further questions
Eliminate some of the possible reasons by Hypothesis (asking questions)
Try a reformulation

© London Borough of Tower Hamlets Educational Psychology Service

26

A **The child is learning more slowly because of basic factors to do with language development and / or task demands.**

CONSIDER:

- the child may be learning more slowly because of limited experience in English. [Remember the timescale involved in second language development. Note the implications from the research on bilingual pupils listed in Chapter 2]

- how long has the child been in school / exposed to English?

- the child may not be learning because basic proficiency in any language is not established and neither language has been given an adequate opportunity to develop. [Remember that first language skills are a valuable means of supporting a child's learning]

- the child may not be learning because the level of basic conversational English has misled the teacher into setting tasks which are too abstract for the child's current language level. [See the model based on the work of Cummins (1984) in Chapter 6]

DISREGARD IF:

- the child has been at school in this country and learning English for more than 5 years.

- there is an unusual pattern or structure to the child's language development. [See Hypothesis 3]

- the child is supported by home language teaching and is reportedly making good progress.

- the child's first language seems as well developed as for other bilingual children from the community of the same age.

- context embedded, concrete learning experiences are frequently provided within the classroom and the child can understand and express themselves well in relation to them.

B **The child is not learning because of environmental stress experienced inside or outside school.**

CONSIDER:

- is the child experiencing the ethos and curriculum of the school as alien and challenging rather than welcoming and accommodating?

- is the child or family experiencing overt or covert racism at home or at school?

- there may be trauma in the case of refugee children who have recent experience of horrific events, e.g. civil war or family separation and bereavement.

- is the child being rejected by others or being subjected to conflicting demands from parents and peers?

- is the family under particular stress due to housing or financial difficulties?

DISREGARD IF:

- the school has a strong multicultural approach to teaching and there is evidence within it of the value placed on the languages and cultural backgrounds of all its pupils.

- there are good staff-parent, staff-pupil, pupil-pupil and school-community relationships together with a lot of contact with adult home language speakers.

- the child seems to have good self esteem; is happy, supported and well motivated.

- there is no evidence of specific racist incidents.
  (Check with parents if you suspect this may be the case)

C The child is failing because of a specific language disorder.

CONSIDER:

- the sequence in which the child is acquiring language compared with the stages of second language learning and the order in which children normally acquire this.

- the ways in which both languages are used to and by the child in various oral situations.

- the evidence of a bilingual speaker on the child's expressive and receptive skills in first language.

- the pragmatic language skills of the child.

DISREGARD IF:

- the child is experiencing a loss of contact with their first/home language.

- the child has only been exposed to English for a short time (up to 6 months).

- no advantage is found in using non-verbal methods in systematic attempts to teach the child concepts.

NB: *Only a very small percentage of children are statistically likely to have a specific language disorder (less than one per cent)*

D The child has Special Educational Needs as defined by the 1981 and 1993 Education Acts.

CONSIDER:

- the information on the child's learning over time.

- the child's learning and language profile and information on the strategies used by the child across the curriculum .

- how much of the curriculum is context embedded?

DISREGARD IF:

- there are a number of other factors which might explain the child's failure to learn apart from lack of ability or specific learning difficulty.

....

WHY DO IT?

- There is a better chance of accurate and well informed assessment when more questions are posed and when greater evidence is collected.

- It is a method which could give a structure to an 'early warning' or 'concern' meeting at which teachers are sharing their concern about an individual child's lack of learning progress.

- It will mean that the focus is on looking at the learning environment as much as at the child.

- Simpler reasons are unlikely to be overlooked.

- The child is less likely to be inaccurately labelled.

HOW TO DO IT

- Work through the listed possible hypotheses for the child's perceived learning difficulties.

- Note down information gathered during the exercise together with areas where answers are unknown or where further information is required.

- Also note down any information and evidence that would appear to rule out the hypothesis.

- Work with colleagues as a brainstorming session. You will stimulate each others thinking!

- Add any other hypotheses or issues pertinent to your school or the child's situation that you feel have not been included or previously checked.

5 Collecting the evidence

In this chapter I am proposing that both primary and secondary schools already collect a wealth of information about pupils learning in many ways. Listed below are just some of the ways in which evidence may be collected about bilingual pupils in your school. It is not inclusive, there are many other systems in use in schools, for example, many primary schools use the Primary Learning Record (Barrs et al 1990)

ASSESSING LANGUAGE STAGES

WHAT ARE THEY?

'Language stages' in today's terminology are largely derived from the work of Hilary Hester and Inner London colleagues at CLPE and first appeared in the Primary Language Record Handbook (Barrs et al 1988). The Home Office had made very specific requirements for the monitoring of the revamped funding for Section 11 projects from 1992 and many schools use a model based on Hester's four stages of English to identify pupils current levels of English (baseline assessment) and as a means of charting progress across time.

These four stages are described as follows:

- **Stage 1**   **new to English**

- **Stage 2**   **becoming familiar with English**

- **Stage 3**   **becoming confident as a user of English**

- **Stage 4**   **a very fluent user of English in most social and learning contexts**

and are followed by a descriptive paragraph of active statements of observable behaviour typical of a (primary) bilingual pupil at each stage.

ESL teachers may be more familiar with earlier descriptors such as: beginner, elementary, intermediate and advanced as second language textbooks, usually aimed at adult learners, are organised into four stages in this way. These generally correlate with the stages given above.

N.B. It is important that these are not confused with the Code of Practice SEN school based 'stages' 1 -3 where pupils are registered on stages of concern for special educational need. (see Chapter 7)

WHY USE THEM?

The purpose of regularly reviewing pupils' language levels is to monitor expected progress across time in the acquisition of English. Continuous teacher assessment is the best method of doing this. It is important that this is seen as part of the school's assessment recording and reporting procedure in showing pupils' attainment in National Curriculum terms. Reports written in isolation from the body of the mainstream teaching and learning would be limited in value. Where class /subject teachers contribute to these records, they can be used as a diagnostic tool to analyse needs for a future teaching focus. Language stages are also used in many LEAs to provide baseline information for statistical purposes.

The Home Office requirement for an annual review to ensure that Section 11 funding is used to best effect means that some LEAs use internal tests, Standard Assessment Tests or public examination results to compare S11 supported pupils with others. The language stage statistics are used to demonstrate the numbers of bilingual pupils at each stage both in order to show progress and to demonstrate the need for continued funding for their support. This can be viewed as somewhat of a contradiction in terms! However the results of these analyses are useful to target additional language support more precisely to student need within an individual institution and also provide discussion/moderation between schools.

HOW TO ASSESS LANGUAGE ACQUISITION

Use the Hester stages as a guide for discussion with colleagues, together with your knowledge of National Curriculum expectations and experience of bilingual pupils normative acquisition of English.

- Design a method of recording progress that fits/is complementary with the current system within the school. (No-one will welcome additional/separate systems!) Continuous teacher assessment and some structured and systematic targeting will focus teaching on aspects which need attention within the curricular framework.

- Create a forum for debate about the nature and expectation of language across the curriculum, subject specific language and appropriate methodologies which will involve bilingual pupils in language activities.

Teachers and departments supporting bilingual learners at secondary schools often have considerable experience and knowledge of patterns of typical errors made by bilingual pupils from one language community. These relate to the structural differences of the first language. An example of an information sheet for Bengali is included as a model. (see Figure overpage) Similar information could be collected, checked with the minority language speakers for accuracy, and distributed to staff in your school/authority. The errors made by most bilingual pupils are likely to fit this pattern and will give you a 'norm'. If a pupil's errors widely deviate from this then further investigation should be made as it may be indicative of a specific disorder.

As we have seen, the whole subject of assessment is fraught with difficulty. There have been many local developments in methods of assessing bilingual pupils' stages of English. The descriptive nature of the Hester stages caused anxiety to many LEAs precisely because of their (deliberate!) imprecision in 'structural' language terms. Many Section 11 project teams have attempted to use the stages to describe bilingual pupils' English language behaviour more objectively. In my own authority this was largely an exercise to ensure an agreed consensus among subject departments and between secondary schools. It was also necessary to

TYPICAL ERRORS
IN ENGLISH MADE BY BENGALI OR SYLHETI SPEAKERS

These North Indian/Bangladeshi languages are derived from Sanskrit and belong to the Indo Ayrian language group.

Children learning to speak English as their second language will often display errors which occur as a result of applying grammatical [syntactical] rules of their home/first language to English.

These structural errors are transient and on their own do **not** mean that the child has a language disorder. However if the errors continue beyond a couple of years and there is other evidence of difficulty in receptive and expressive language a child may need to assessed by the Speech and Language Service. [These difficulties would also be evident in L1 so a bilingual assessment is desirable]

As children become more competent in English they will also make errors that are typical, common, developmental errors of monolingual children, particularly in use of grammatical rules.

GRAMMATICAL DIFFERENCES

● The basic word order in a sentence is **subject - object - verb** [SOV] compared to the English order of SVO.

● There is no definite [the] or indefinite article [a] before the noun.

● Post positions are used instead of prepositions.

● The third person pronoun is the same for masculine and feminine gender. Verb inflection usually signals gender.

● A second form of the second person pronoun is used with elders/strangers as a mark of respect.

● Bengali uses gender for neutral/natural nouns e.g. sun [masculine]; moon,river [feminine].

● The verb component of a sentence can consist of one, two or three parts. The first part of the verb is in root form which inflection to signify tense.

● Adverbs usually precede the noun.

TYPICAL ERRORS

- Putting verbs at the end of sentences.
  "He crayons not giving"

- Leaving out articles before a noun.
  "She give me sweet"

- Using prepositions after a noun or inserting them where unnecessary.
  "I told to my mum"

- Confusing placement of plurals especially noun-adjective concord.
  "bigs girls"

- Incorrect use of third person pronouns, particularly overuse of
  "he", "him"

- Inappropriate use of 'no'; 'not' .
  "He no play with me", "I not got my pencil"

- Omitting auxiliary verb.
  "My dad going Bangladesh", "He reading"

- Placing adverbs or adverbial phrases inappropriately.
  "He too much cursing"

- Wrong use [or lack] of preposition.
  "He hit me in my arm"

N.B.

- *Bengali writing **hangs** on the line while English writing **sits** on the line.*

- *Bengali script does not distinguish between capital and lower case letters.*

ensure consistency across the Borough for statistical purposes. The exercise proved that there was a remarkable degree of agreement, in fact. The precise wording caused more difficulty largely because individual schools had developed their own banks of statements which they were reluctant to compromise or jettison for a common system.

Most of the 'local' stage models have separated each stage into the four language skills of National Curriculum English; reading, writing, speaking and listening. The latter two are often amalgamated. The secondary framework for assessment eventually agreed upon locally was of particular benefit to those newly in post or where schools had not yet developed strong systems. It was particularly pleasing that the framework was flexible enough to be used in various ways by departments in different schools after a period of piloting with new Year 7 intakes. Three examples follow:

- School 1 used the statement bank to create an A4 fourfold recording sheet for every targeted bilingual pupil where statements were 'highlighted' in a different colour each term to show progress at a glance. *(see pages 35,36 &37)*

- School 2 used the proforma as an INSET tool with a subject department which provided some discussion, training and considerable awareness-raising about language activities and achievement within the subject area.

- School 3 put the statement bank onto their department/school computer network which is updated termly.

There are many local variations of such assessment forms. Check with your own authority.

Assessment of·bilingual learners

Language Assessment Log E.S.L. Department

SCHOOL : _____

Name and Surname : _____

Tutor Group : _____

Date of Entry into School : _____

Years of Schooling in Britain : _____

First Language : _____

Date of Assessment / Colour Code :

199 _____ Autumn Term _____ Orange _____

Spring Term _____ Green _____

Summer Term _____ Yellow _____

Curriculum area subject /through which language development is assessed :

_____

Assessment completed by _____ *(Teachers name)*
:

35

Assessment of (secondary) bilingual learners

STAGE ONE

Listening	Speaking	Reading	Writing
a) Listens and responds to: questions commands instruction in L1 non-verbally	a) is silent in class b) speaks predominantly in first langauge c) initiates single words short phrases asks simple questions	a) recognises letters b) sounds out words c) reads simple words d) recognises words in context e) relies on pictures for meaning f) reads for meaning	a) forms letters b) attempts task via copying c) remembers spelling of some basic words d) spells phonetically e) relies on structure of given model f) begins to write independently.

STAGE TWO

Listening	Speaking	Reading	Writing
a) still requires reiterration of instructions b) can retrieve specific information from teacher/ group talk c) follows simple instructions and explanations	a) converses in informal situations b) begins to participate in group work	a) retrieves specific information from passage b) attempts unknown words c) begins to guess meaning of unknown words from context d) able to read and discuss text	a) begins to punctuate b) can write short passages using prompts as guide c) shows some understanding of spelling patterns d) can sequence work in a logical order e) shows awareness of rule system e.g. tenses

STAGE THREE

Listening	Speaking	Reading	Writing
a) clearly understands great amount of teacher and peer talk b) followes complex explanations c) needs less support in comprehension and execution of tasks required	a) shows confidence in initiation and sustaining a conversation b) shows confidence about reporting back in different situations c) beginning to vary language according to audience d) performs broad range of language functions such as questioning and predicting e) use of spoken language is still in advance of literacy	a) reads more complex texts with much understanding b) manages with mainstream materials but may still require some support c) reads aloud with speed, confidence and fluency but not always with appropriate expression	a) can write independently although writing may still show errors in: specific vocabulary spelling and punctuation grammatical relationships b) attempts to express complex ideas but clarity often blurred by above areas c) beginning to develop appropriate styles and registers d) is aware of linguistic limitations and occasionally frustrated by them

STAGE FOUR

Listening	Speaking	Reading	Writing
a) fluent bilingual		a) able to read a range of materials confidently b) able to skim and scan	a) can confidently undertake a range of different types of writing b) shows influence of extended reading when writing

LANGUAGE STAGE

LEVEL		Speaking	Listening	Reading	Writing
	Beginner				
	1				
	2				
	3				
	4				

ASSESSING FIRST LANGUAGE DEVELOPMENT

WHAT IS IT?

Most schools give pupils who speak a home language other than English and who are new to the school or new to English some sort of internally designed initial assessment test. This is widely agreed to be helpful in establishing the learner's competence in English and provides a basis for immediate and future additional teaching. It can identify areas for development and establish short or longer term targets by identifying what a child knows, understands and can do in addition to their current competence in English. Such tests are vital where a child is admitted to school as a 'casual entry' but less necessary where a child transfers with records and samples of work from another local school. Some of the dangers of assessing English can be minimised if the assessment can be carried out with the help of a trained mother tongue speaker.

Some young children who have been born in the UK have been exposed to little or no English before school. A first language assessment can be particularly useful in diagnosing language difficulty for those pupils whose learning progress is already causing concern compared with other bilingual peers from a similar background. Assessing children in their mother tongue can also help to sort out whether the lack of adequate progress is to do with the acquisition of a second language or whether conceptual or information processing difficulties are present. It can work as an indicator to guide monolingual teachers in arranging more appropriate support for diagnosed difficulties

WHY DO IT?

Many schools/LEAs employ bilingual assistants as mother tongue speakers. They can be trained and supported to administer a school developed test in a child's first language. Where a young child's learning is causing concern, this would help to establish whether the child's first language is delayed or poorly developed. If this is the case, remediation can be given by the bilingual assistant using both languages and progress closely monitored by the teacher. This is a valuable and focussed use of their skills in the classroom.

- Poorly developed L1 may be an important indicator of special educational needs.In any case, a child whose first language is not well developed by school age will be severely disadvantaged in learning a second language and targeted support could prevent learning failure at a critical early stage.

HOW TO ASSESS FIRST LANGUAGE

- Items which can assess the child's first language communication skills in terms of the expectations of normal classroom language activities such as retelling stories, sequencing pictures, listening and acting upon simple instructions will also give information on the use of linguistic structures such as tense. If similar material has been trialled with bilingual children of the same age and background within the

38

school who are making good progress in their learning then some local norms will quickly be established.

- Use of a tape recording of the children's' performance can be invaluable for discussion, trialling agreement and training purposes with colleagues.

- Using a bilingual member of staff who is familiar to the children and who has worked in the classroom will be less threatening to the child being assessed. It is also important to note when and to what extent the child was prompted, together with affective factors such as whether the child seemed anxious, unwell, confidant and so on.

A model of a first oral language assessment form is included here as an example of one primary school's work in this field. [see Figure overpage] It was developed and trialled over the course of two terms by a working party consisting of the deputy head (also the SEN co-ordinator); the school Section 11 coordinator; the bilingual instructor; the Reading Recovery trained teacher and myself. It also involved discussion with the school's EP; the Principal EP; a bilingual assessment teacher and the local Speech and Language service. It is offered here, not as a definitive assessment test but as an example of the sort of assessment which can be developed to suit local needs. The materials for the test are two Brian Wildsmith's picture story books without words; 'The Nest' and 'The Apple Bird' copies of which are in the classroom and familiar to the pupils, and some everyday objects common to both cultures.

The school is using the test to assess and work intensively with Yr 1 &2 children causing concern in three ways.

- Some have been found to have poorly developed first language skills and the bilingual instructor is working with the children and their families to provide additional first language support.

- Others have been assessed as having satisfactory or good mother tongue skills. These are then targeted by the Section 11 teachers for more structured help in acquiring English.

- Some children show weaknesses in certain of the assessed areas. They are subsequently included in small group activities to remediate these.

First Language Assessment

SCHOOL : _____

Children causing concern : First Language Assessment Year 1/2
Remember to praise child after each task!

Name : _____ **Year :** _____ **Date of Birth :** _____

Date : _____ **Assessed by :** _____

Task 1   Narrative (The Nest)

"Look at these pictures. They tell a story.
Can you tell me what is happening?"
PROMPT....   "What is happening here? Tell me."

Good	Ok	Poor	Prompt

Comments :

Task 2   Sequencing (The Applebird)

"These pictures make a story too.
They are all muddled up.
Can you put them in order to tell a story?"
PROMPT....   "Which picture do you think comes first?"
*   "Which picture comes next?"*

Left to right ? [ ]

Comments :

Task 3   Relating personal experience

"Tell me what you did...   in class this morning."
(at home last night,
before you come to school this morning,
in the playground at break)

Good	Ok	Poor	Prompt

Comments :

40

Task 4   Comprehension

"Now we are going to do something different. I am going to ask you to give me something from the things on the table. Listen carefully to what I ask you to do. Are you ready ..... (Child's name)...?

"Give me the thing I need .... to open the door
What did you give me?"   key

"Give me the thing I need .... to eat my food
What did you give me?"   spoon

"Give me the thing I need .... to write in my book
What did you give me?"   pen

"Give me the thing I need .... to cut paper
What did you give me?"   scissors

"Give me the thing I need .... to comb my hair
What did you give me?"   comb

Task 5   Following verbal instructions

"Now I am going to ask you to do something else. Look at the things in front of you. Listen carefully. OK. Ready?

Put the spoon in the jar.
Put the scissors on the floor.
Put the key under your chair.

Put the spoon on the table and the key in the jar.
Put the pen on the chair and the scissors on the table.

Put the spoon in the jar, take the key out of the jar and put the key on top of the scissors.

Take the spoon out of the jar and put the jar on the carpet. Put the pen in the jar."

Task 6   Memory

"I'm going to say some numbers. I want you to repeat them after I've finished "
(Stop when the child has got 2 of them wrong).

2 5	7 3
8 1 6	9 4 5
7 2 9 6	4 1 3 8
6 4 2 1 7	3 9 7 5 8

ADDITIONAL COMMENTS :

Was the child :   nervous   tired   shy   anxious
                    cooperative   confident   unwell   lacking concentration

READING STRATEGIES

WHAT ARE THEY?

As young children develop as readers and their knowledge, experience and understanding of texts increases, they move along a continuum from dependence to independence.(Barrs et al 1988) 'Becoming a reader: Reading Scale 1' suggests a simple way of recording a young child's progress along a dimension from being reliant on an adult reading a text aloud, to greater confidence in deciphering familiar and the unfamiliar texts for themselves. From the same source 'Reading scale 2' gives information about a child's experience as a reader across the curriculum on a separate scale and is useful for older pupils from Year 3 onwards.

Psycholinguists describe the range of cue systems in the English language as follows:

- semantic cues - using previous knowledge of stories and texts to predict w o r d s, events, phrases which are likely to make the text make sense; i.e. 'meaning' cues.

- syntactic cues - relying on knowledge and experience of patterns in spoken and written language (grammar) to predict text; i.e. structural language cues.

- grapho-phonic cues - applying knowledge and experience of the relationships between sounds and symbols to decipher particular words; i.e. print cues.

Experienced readers apply a combination of these strategies in order to read. Clay (1979) claims that "all readers, from five year old beginners on their first books to the effective adult reader need to use: the meaning; the sentence structure; order cues; size cues; special features; special knowledge; first and last letter cues before they resort to left to right sounding out chunks or letter clusters, or in the last resort, single letters. Such an analysis makes the terms 'look and say' or 'sight words' or 'phonics' nonsense as explanations of what we need to know or do in order to be able to read." Weaver (1980) shows how these strategies are combined in a process which follows a repeating cycle of : prediction, sampling, confirming and correcting. Reading is clearly more than just a sum of its parts even when there is agreement as to what these parts are and readers need to experience a wide range of texts to achieve critical literacy.

WHY ARE THEY IMPORTANT?

Knowledge of the strategies employed by the child will usefully inform the teacher as to where appropriate support can be given to aid understanding and fluency when reading. This is important for bilingual pupils in learning English as they may be gaining literacy in more than one language. The dependence-independence and inexperienced-experience scales (Barrs et al 1988) would give useful information about knowledge of language other than English especially if noted by a bilingual teacher who shares the child's home language. Noting the reading strategies employed by the child would also help to prevent the phenomena frequently observed in the lower secondary school whereby pupils appear to decipher unseen print with fluency yet understand little of the text which they are 'reading'. Awareness of the individual reading style of the pupil means that support can be focussed on the nature of the learning task.

'Miscue Analysis" is a method of analysing what children do as they read an unseen text aloud. It is based on the work of Goodman (1973) and has been subsequently adapted by others (including Barrs et al 1988) as a way of recording the errors and self corrections made by the child as s/he processes the text. The successful strategies used when reading can then be identified together with the negative strategies which may be hindering a general understanding of the text. The only difference in approach for a bilingual child might be the focus on the degree of structure, detail, systematic teaching and continuous assessment/ record keeping in activities which emphasise meaning. It is preferable to work from a familiar or discussed text as in 'Reading Recovery'.

'Reading Recovery' is an individual teaching programme for the early detection of reading difficulties based on the work of Marie Clay (1979). It is usually offered to young pupils of approximately six years, selected for additional support by trained, supervised teachers. Part of the teacher's time is funded specifically for the systematic observation and teaching programme as part of a school's committment to reducing reading difficulties. Twenty six authorities in Britain have funding for official Reading Recovery schemes, however the term is sometimes used in a more generalised (and unofficial)way for less rigorous programmes. The reason for mentioning it here is that it provides very detailed and closely monitored information on the child's reading, writing and spelling strategies. If a bilingual pupil has been selected for this individual teaching, usually thirty minutes daily, the very full information yielded will be a valuable part of any assessment of literacy.

'THRIVE' (*Tower Hamlets Reading Initiative Via Exploration*) is a local initiative of early literacy screening for whole classes in years 2 or 3. It involves three visits, one each term, from a specialist literacy teacher and aims to screen those pupils experiencing difficulty; to support the classteacher with appropriate focused strategies and to monitor progress across the year. Pupils who are left on the concern list at the end of the year will be considered for registration of special educational needs at stage 2. THRIVE is a typical example of early screening programmes developed in the 1970's and 1980's by many authorities to assess a cohort of young children. Early intervention using systematic observation is recognised as of key importance in preventing literacy difficulties and information yielded about the strategies used by a bilingual pupil is important evidence.

SAMPLES OF WORK: PUPIL PROFILES

WHAT ARE THEY?

An experienced teacher can often tell a great deal more about a child's level of learning from an annotated piece of work than from detailed reports. Unfortunately teachers have not always been encouraged to trust their years of experience which, in fact, gives them many benchmarks against which to judge learning performance more reliably than a single test result. In the same way, samples of a pupil's work taken across time and across the curriculum can be more revealing than standardised test results.

The 'Records of Achievement" movement for secondary pupils aimed to record pupil's success in all aspects of their school life not merely academic success. Pupils leaving school at the end of their statutory school life, sometimes with little in the way of exam results were able to take with them a record which included samples of work.

In the same way as continuous teacher assessment records learning development across time, so portfolios, profiles and work samples can map the development of pupil's learning in English as a second language. At a recent local INSET session to 'moderate' language stages at secondary stage, teachers brought in samples of pupils' work from different curriculum areas which they felt was representative of Stages 1 to 4. This led to very useful discussion about standard errors and the skills demanded for ' extended writing' in humanities at Key Stage 4 among other issues.

WHY DO IT?

A pupil 'profile' or collection of samples of work is intended to demonstrate progress across time. This gives important information about:

- rate(speed) of progress

- types of errors being made

- familiarity with the variety of written forms demanded by different curriculum areas.

This information can be used diagnostically to inform teachers how to target support. and can help teachers to observe when a plateau of learning occurs (usually Stage2 or 3) so that they can minimise educational underachievement in pupils who would be capable of better results at the end of Key Stage 4.

HOW TO COLLECT SAMPLES OF WORK

Many secondary schools have collected samples of coursework to use in moderation exercises. OFSTED inspections expect to see some pupils' work across the curriculum for the school year and profiles of samples of core curriculum work are kept as a matter of course by many primary schools as part of their continuous assessment. The method for keeping the work is as various as the institutions involved, the main point is for clarity and agreement about:

- what to keep?

- how to annotate it (date, subject, first draft, corrected, unaided, with support?)

- how it is to be stored (so that it is accessible, where and in what container?)

- how often to sample?

- why is it being done (relationship to assessment, recording and reporting?)

44

PUPIL SELF ASSESSMENT

WHAT IS IT?

This is related to the above section as pupils should be closely involved in the monitoring and selection of their work samples.

WHY ENCOURAGE THIS?

Involving pupils in some responsibility for their own learning is more likely to lead to better motivation for intrinsic rewards and greater independnce. As pupils learn a greater self reliance by negotiating and taking pride in their learning, their involvement in objective self assessment can empower them as learners. Even young pupils are capable of evaluating their work, reflecting on their own progress and acknowledging strengths and weaknesses.

HOW TO DO IT

● build this into your reporting and recording systems

● use self assessment sheets at the end of lessons/units of work (see Figure overpage)

● through 'conferencing' (a structured, recorded meeting of pupil and teacher)

NB *The Code of Practice (DFE 1994) sets an expectation that older pupils at stage 2 or 3 on the schools SEN register should be 'consulted' in the writing and review of the 'individual education plans' made for them!*

School records / assessments

WHAT ARE THEY?

These are the systems in place in schools which OFSTED inspectors will examine for evidence of the methods used for pupils' 'assessment, recording and reporting' (known as AR&R). There is often a mass of information about bilingual pupils' learning in different parts of the school's record systems which, if put together in one place, would provide comprehensive evidence of whether there was cause for concern of special educational needs.

WHY DO IT?

Some of these are legal requirements;

● School records must be kept on every pupil's progress and these must be updated at least once a year.

● Schools must provide a written report to parents at least once a year, including National Curriculum assessments.

● Pupils' achievements in public examinations must be made available for publication.

Self Assessment Sheet

Topic .... Subject ....

Name .... Class ....

The work I enjoyed doing most was ....
....

because ....

I think I do best when ....
....

because ....

The work I am most proud of is ....
....

because ....

The work I found most difficult was ....
....

because ....

I think I am quite good at these skills ....
....

because ....

I think I need to work on these skills ....
....

Signature .... Date ....

46

- Schools are required to assess National Curriculum subjects at or near the end of each Key Stage.

  Apart from these, school records measure the progress of bilingual pupils compared to their peers. The amount of time spent in learning English is a key factor in the consideration which need to be given to the pupil's learning needs.

HOW TO DO IT

A look at the Handbook for the Inspection of Schools (OFSTED 1994) sets expectations about this:

- whatever the individual arrangements made by the school, they need to be manageable!

- the outcomes need to inform future work and be written in a way which is constructive and helpful to teachers, pupils and their parents

- the school's arrangements for AR&R will result in accurate and consistent records of achievement of individual pupils in relation to NC attainment targets.

NATIONAL CURRICULUM ASSESSMENTS

WHAT ARE THEY?

These consist of teacher assessments of the National Curriculum foundation subjects as to the Levels of Attainment (ATs) demonstrated by the pupils on the Programmes of Study (PoS) laid down. (These are currently still under some review as a result of the Dearing Report 1994). Pupils are also to be assessed by standard national tests, previously known as standard assessment tests (SATs). The latter are externally prescribed and set across the country at the same time to pupils of similar ages at the end of the four Key Stages. These are to be set at age seven (Year 2); age eleven (Year 6); age fourteen (Year 9) and age sixteen (Year 11). Partial testing has so far been carried out at KS1 and KS3 as political action by teachers meant that many children were not tested in 1993 and 1994.

WHY DO IT?

You have no choice! Schools are required to assess pupils in NC subjects under the Education Reform Act (DFE 1988) Guidance is set out in various DFE Circulars from subsequent years. As this is mandatory it is important that whatever systems are in place for the assessment of bilingual pupils fit with this requirement in order to :

- involve curriculum members of staff

- minimise additional workloads

- ensure that bilingual pupils are assessed as part of mainstream curriculum

47

HOW TO DO IT

We know that assessment and testing of any child is complex and controversial. The central issue for bilingual pupils revolves around the question of how any assessment can be fair and accurate if conducted in a language that is not familiar to the child. The real challenge is how to overcome the gap between what the child knows and is capable of and her/his performance in a second language which may act as a barrier to a demonstration of achievement. One solution would be to assess the child in the first language and the DFE has conceded that 'special arrangements' may be made for Standard National Tests whereby :

● a trained mother tongue support teacher, fluent in the child's first language, can help with the assessments for science and maths. They may provide oral translation of certain words or phrases and simplify the written instructions in line with the 'Test Guidance Notes' distributed to schools.

● pupils may, at the head teacher's discretion use bilingual dictionaries or word lists as long as these do not provide any subject assistance i.e. they cannot be used for English tests.

6 Planning Support

All schools have a duty to support the learning of all their pupils, acknowledging individual differences and learning needs in their planning and provision. For bilingual pupils, much support is proffered through the methodologies and good practice considered earlier in this handbook. In this chapter another method of supporting individual pupils is offered together with a suggestion of one planning tool for differentiation which has particular relevance for bilingual pupils whose learning is causing concern.

INDIVIDUAL ACTION PLANS

WHAT ARE THEY?

Individual action plans have long been used by special educational needs teachers to plan and monitor specific interventions with pupils who are giving cause for concern. These have now become a formal part of the guidance for SEN at school based Stages 2 &3 in the Code of Practice (DFE 1994) renamed as Individual Education Plans (IEPs) The production of this plan characterises Stage 2 and should set out:

- the nature of the learning difficulties.

- the intended action or provision, staff involved, frequency of intervention and specific programme. activities, materials

- help/support from parents at home

- time constrained targets

- monitoring and assessment arrangements

- review arrangements and date (usually within a term)

However an Individual Action Plan (NB this term should distinguish it from any direct association with SEN) can be written for any pupil by any teacher wherever there is a need to focus some short term additional support for learning for a pupil. It is simply a systematic action plan based on teachers' skills of observation agreed with the pupil concerned.

WHY USE THEM ?

The reality of most classrooms is for pupils to work in groups, however for the exceptional case where a pupil does not seem to be making the expected progress, an Action Plan can help pinpoint the problem. The emphasis on a systematic approach automatically means that some focussed thinking, planning and action is likely to occur. Most pupils would benefit from this, though the majority of bilingual pupils will not require it. Bilingual pupils causing learning concern should make accelerated progress as a result of a specific action plan if it is properly executed. Those who don't may have some greater difficulty which will need to be referred. (See example overleaf.)

Individual Action Plan

For ....   start date ....

Class ....   review date ....

Area of work

Evidence

Plan

Action Taken

Individual Action Plan (teachers' notes)

For ....   start date ....

Class ....   review date ....

Area of work

involve pupil if possible

- clarify and define problem
- pin it down to a specific area of curriculum, skill and activity
- specify the difficulty as clearly as possible

Evidence

involve pupil if possible

- Define present level of skill in area
- What can pupil do/not do?
- What strategies does pupil use?
- What are pupil's strengths?

Plan

involve pupil in decisions

- Write down exactly what you intend pupil to do
- (make it small steps, observable and measurable)
- When will it happen? (daily? twice a week? when)
- For how long? how often?
- Where?
- Who will help pupil? (teacher? helper? group? peer?)

Action Taken

- Use this space to record any outcomes, problems, changes made
- Report back at review with evidence of pupil's learning during 'Action Plan' period.

HOW TO USE THEM

Individual Action Plans can be used as a systematic approach for any pupil causing concern by any teacher following this plan. It is particularly useful if you work with a colleague:

● clarify and define the problem using your skills of observation and reflection

● collect evidence about the concern (what can the pupil do and not do?)

● plan what to do, when and who will do it; set achievable targets

● act on it

● review progress, refocus targets

NB *Action plans of any sort need to be 'SMART' i.e:*

S   Specific
M   Measurable
A   Attainable
R   Relevant
T   Time-constrained

DIFFERENTIATING THE CURRICULUM

WHAT IS IT?

There has been much recent emphasis on differentiation. In fact it has become one of the educational' buzzwords of the seventies, *"used by many, understood by some and put fully into practice by a few"*. (Visser 1993) It is certainly an aspect of teaching which receives the attention of an OFSTED inspection who are looking for evidence of *"the matching of work to the differing capabilities of individuals or groups of pupils in order to extend their learning"*. (OFSTED 1993)

It is a process which should ensure that the curriculum offer is appropriate and motivating for all pupils by an equal emphasis on the component parts of curriculum i.e.; methodology, organisation and content. The three most challenging groups of pupils in a mixed ability classroom in this respect are bilingual pupils, very able ('gifted') pupils and those with special educational needs.

WHY DO IT?

Apart from the OFSTED expectation, teachers need some understanding of differentiation to ensure that all pupils have access to the curriculum. This is their entitlement to an equal opportunity to reach their learning potential. Bilingual pupils are capable of high achievement if appropriate demands, materials and methodology are employed in the classroom.

If differentiation is seen as a concern to meet the learning needs of all pupils within the classroom, then it is inevitable that some schools /teachers will respond solely in terms of pupils cognitive ability. The solution to this is frequently seen in terms of 'setting', 'banding' or streaming by ability. For pupils whose first language is other than English there are equal opportunity issues of language access. They may well be pupils of considerable cognitive ability who need help to demonstrate mastery of concepts in a second language. However they are unlikely to be placed with others of their own ability because of their limited command of English. An emphasis on pupil diversity seen in terms of ability, age and aptitude does not actually give pupils more homegeneity of attitudes, beliefs or values. In fact, it could be said to enhance division and differences. Differentiation should mean that the curriculum offer is both appropriate and motivating for all pupils and this has a role to play in sustaining positive pupil behaviour at school.

HOW TO DO IT?

There are many models of differentiation. Some suggest that curriculum can be differentiated by task so that the teacher sets different tasks within a common area of study. However, factors which affect the difficulty of a task include a pupil's familiarity with the materials, concepts and language used and the extent to which models, prompts and concrete referrants are made available. Differentiation by outcome involves setting a common task on the assumption that pupils' learning outcomes will vary according to their individual aptitudes and interests. Well planned and lively stimuli should motivate pupils to work to their maximum potential. More able pupils could be expected to use more difficult concepts, carry out more complex operations and express their learning in more sophisticated language rather than just produce 'more'. (John Visser's recent publication (1993) is a useful guide to staff development on differentiation)

One of the most important aims of differentiation is to help pupils take an increasingly greater responsibility for their own learning. The following matrix of Jim Cummins (1984) is offered as a helpful way of thinking about the learning needs of different groups of pupils so that they can operate more autonomously in the classroom.

CURRICULUM RELATED ASSESSMENT : THE CUMMINS FRAMEWORK (see pages 55-56)

WHAT IS IT?

In recent years, emphasis has been placed on curriculum based assessment with bilingual pupils as it has been viewed as a less discriminatory alternative than the standardised measures of psychological tests or casual observation. However, applying the behavioural methodology of direct instruction, task analysis and precision teaching have serious disadvantages in assessing bilingual children.

In a leading publication on this subject, Jim Cummins (1984) expressed serious reservations of the model of curriculum based assessment most commonly used by British psychologists. He pointed out several arguments against using a direct instruction approach with bilingual children. An emphasis on teacher initiation and control may actually inhibit the active involvement of the child which linguists argue are necessary for the development of cognitive academic language proficiency. He also argues powerfully against the reduction of meaningful context which often results from task analysis where learning is broken down into isolated parts. One of the best ways of assisting bilingual pupils is to ensure that the knowledge or skill to be taught is embedded in a comprehensible and meaningful learning context.

The term 'curriculum related assessment' (CRA) has come to mean any method of assessing children which includes directly assessing their performance within the curriculum for the purpose of determining their teaching needs. The Cummins framework is offered here as one model which can be easily used by teachers as a tool for planning and differentiating curriculum. It can also be used as a means of recording learning outcomes by noting observations of positive achievement demonstrated in the classroom directly onto a matrix.

WHY USE IT?

- It is a simple model which is easy to use and understand.

- It fits with the demands of planning and differentiating National Curriculum.

- It considers the needs of three different groups of pupils, i.e.very able pupils; bilingual pupils; special educational needs pupils.

- It should ensure that bilingual children are stretched rather than mindlessly employed through appropriately demanding but comprehensible tasks.

- It puts a focus on raising levels of achievement and teacher expectation through an emphasis on cognitive demand.

HOW TO DO IT?

- Use the two dimensions of the matrix (*See photocopiable sheet on page 55.*) to help you consider:
  a) the particular learning styles, experience, skills and needs of individual pupils
  b) the requirements of the task
  c) the context and situation where the learning will take place

- Work collaboratively with colleagues at the planning stage, especially if you share classroom and teaching responsibilities with other colleagues; bilingual assistants, nursery nurses, language or learning support staff. This will generate ideas and discussion

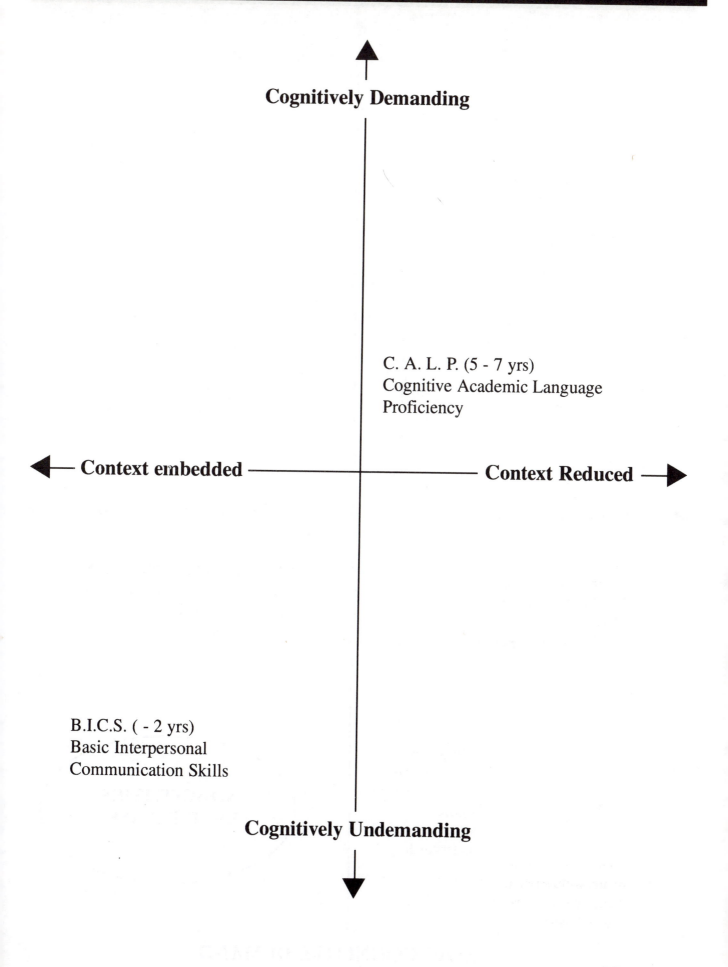

Cognitively Demanding

C. A. L. P. (5 - 7 yrs)
Cognitive Academic Language
Proficiency

Context embedded ──────── **Context Reduced**

B.I.C.S. (- 2 yrs)
Basic Interpersonal
Communication Skills

Cognitively Undemanding

55

HIGH COGNITIVE DEMAND

** bilingual pupils need the majority of their work to be set at this level so that increasing demands are being made on them whilst ensuring understanding through concrete and contextual content and processes

COGNITIVE ACADEMIC LEARNING PROFICIENCY
(acquired in 5 to 7 years)

(bilingual pupils) – – ➤

* * very able pupils must always be given work at this level

◄ **CONTEXT EMBEDDED** ———— **CONTEXT UNEMBEDDED** ➤

BASIC INTERPERSONAL COMMUNICATION SKILLS
(acquired within 2 years)

UNDESIRABLE TERRITORY !
if tasks are both undemanding and abstract they are undesirable in the classroom. What is their learning potential?

bilingual pupils need to move along this axis to ensure achievement with understanding

NO ACTIVITIES HERE PLEASE!

** pupils with learning difficulties need carefully planned work here

LOW COGNITIVE DEMAND

Cognitive Processes: Using the Cummins framework

generalises

compares and **contrasts**

summarises

plans

classifies by known criteria

transforms,personalises given information

recalls and **reviews**

seeks solutions to problems

argues a case using evidence persuasively

identifies criteria,develops and **sustains ideas**

justifies opinion or judgement

evaluates critically

interprets evidence, makes deductions

forms hypotheses, asks further questions for investigation

predicts results

applies principles to new situation

analyses,suggests solution and tests

COGNITIVE PROCESSES

reading to find specific information

- **identifies**
- **names**
- **matches**
- **retells**

transfers information from
one medium to another

applies known procedures

describes observations

sequences

narrates with sense of
beginning,middle,end

- **parrots:** repeats utterances of adult
  or peer

- **copies:** reproduces information from
  board or texts

57

- Start with one unit or aspect of a topic/programme of study you intend to teach. Start small, plot tasks and activities according to the level of cognitive demand and context embeddedness you think are involved.

- Use the worked examples on pages 59 to 63 to help you get started

- Refer to the matrix on page 57 giving examples of cognitive processes (but do bear in mind these are debatable and fairly meaningless when separated from their actual learning contexts)

NOTES ON WORKED EXAMPLES

The examples given on the following pages have been developed at teacher workshops and are intended to get you started on the process of using the Cummins matrix as a tool for your own planning for differentiation. You will come up with your own solutions based on your knowledge of the learning needs of pupils in your classroom.

KSI SCIENCE *(See photocopiable sheet on pages 59 & 60)*

This matrix shows the possible range of pupil responses during a practical activity of 'FLOATING AND SINKING' (this relates to AT1 levels 1, 2a,2b,2c and AT3 levels 1,2 and 3 of the unrevised NC Science orders) This use of the matrix could be used to show pupils' evidence of learning as part of the teachers assessment. This sort of activity is typical of those conceptual areas with which a bilingual child may be very familiar, yet not have sufficient English to demonstrate her/his mastery. The accompanying notes show some ideas for methods of recording which could be used.

KS2 GEOGRAPHY *(See photocopiable sheet on pages 61 & 62)*

This example shows one teacher's attempts to plan a range of differentiated activities for a mixed Year 3 and 4 class on 'THE LOCAL AREA' (AT1 levels 2, 5.1, 5.2 and level 3, 5.1, 5.2 and 5.3) It also includes some practical ideas for materials and methodology

KS3 ENGLISH *(See photocopiable sheet on page 63)*

This example shows the mapping of the activities developed in a pack of materials designed to support the teaching and accessibility of a 'difficult text' Shakespeare's 'ROMEO AND JULIET' (Field 1992) The materials were developed in collaboration with Stuart Scott and the Collaborative Learning Project, trialled in local schools and represent a methodology and activities which could be adapted to any text. The pack is available with others from the Language Support Service LBTH (see Useful Addresses) The use of these materials is also discussed more fully in Hall (1994)

Cognitively Demanding

Evidence of Learning

- makes predictions about other objects (in classroom) which might float/sink

- can state why they think objects sink or float

- sorts objects by other qualities e.g. heavy/light wood/metal

- can suggest questions/ideas based on everyday experience which can be tested

- can predict other objects (not present) which would float/sink

- can make series of related observations

- uses observations to compare expected out come with that observed and make conclusions

◄ **Context embedded** ——— KS1 SCIENCE — **Context Reduced** ►

AT1, L1, 2 abc
AT3 L1,2,3

FLOATING & SINKING

- sorts objects into sets - 'these sink' - 'these float'

- water play: child states 'this sinks'; 'this floats'

Entry Lang. Skills

Preteach: on, under; floats, sinks; object names e.g. scissors, cork etc.

Cognitively Undemanding

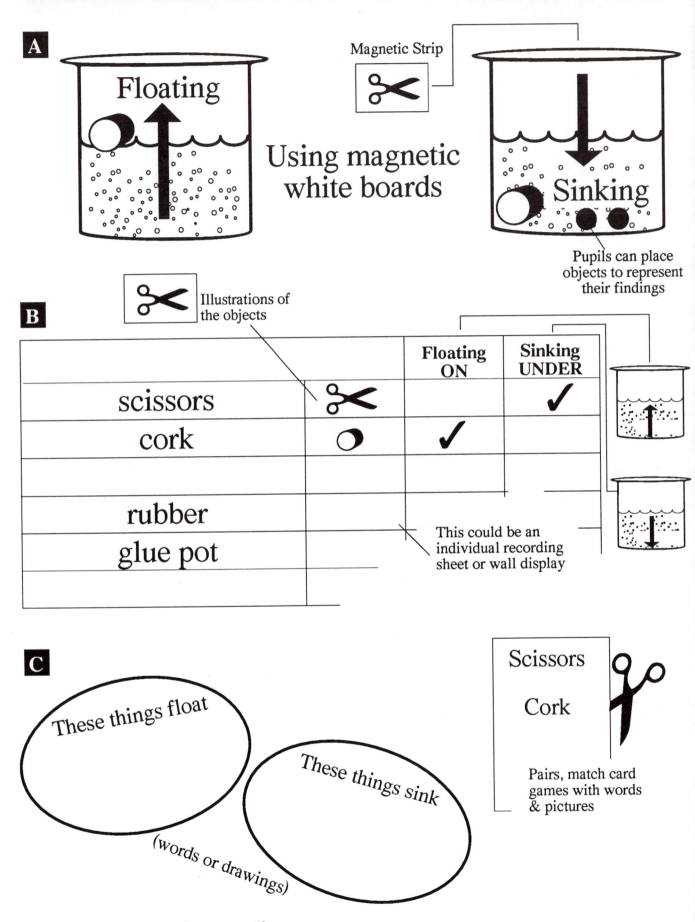

A

Floating

Using magnetic white boards

Magnetic Strip

Sinking

Pupils can place objects to represent their findings

B

Illustrations of the objects

		Floating ON	Sinking UNDER
scissors	✂		✔
cork	○	✔	
rubber			
glue pot			

This could be an individual recording sheet or wall display

C

These things float

These things sink

(words or drawings)

Scissors

Cork

Pairs, match card games with words & pictures

Making sets & recording

60

HIGH COGNITIVE DEMAND

Computer: 'directions'
(Smile - The next 17)

using coordinates to describe/find features on map

aerial photo and map - plot on places of interest using colour key (e.g. green = park)

design key symbols for features - (compare with O.S.)

using vocabulary bank connect photo to name to position on map

design routes (treasure hunt) with written instructions for other groups using geog. vocabulary

GEOG KS2

posing questions and answers about why certain features are where

CONTEXT EMBEDDED

CONTEXT UNEMBEDDED

LOCAL AREA

AT 1 L2. S1, S2
L3, S1,S2, S3
YRS 3 + 4

using aerial photo to trace routes

walking local area identifying features matching photos and names (and in Bengali script)

computer: "pip" - obstacle course

"ship to shore" using N.S.E.W./ obstacle course using left and right as part of P.E. activity in school hall/ gym. (Use correct compass points for walls!)

LOW COGNITIVE DEMAND

A

photo

church — label

গীর্জা

B

mosque

park

BOW
underground station

C

Vocabulary Bank

(using pictures where possible - 'glossary' listed alphabetically)

D

North
উত্তর

West
পশ্চিম

East
পূর্ব

দক্ষিণ
South

'Ship to Shore' labels

HIGH COGNITIVE DEMAND

prologue

using pictorial clues to match and sequence couplets from prologue

character

'2 minute autobiographies' using cards

* text*

"quote quest: matching quotations to statements about character

prologue

modern English version matched to text

prologue

modern English version matched with story

prologue

sequencing prologue couplets (without clues)

character

research using blank cards/devise quiz game using information from text.

text

'filling the gaps' using speeches from key scenes and full text to research before and after

theme

'who was to blame?'prepare debate for tribunal or discursive essay

◀ CONTEXT EMBEDDED ——— CONTEXT UNEMBEDDED ▶

character

'connect four': statement about character

Romeo & Juliet
ENGLISH K.S.3

story

' summary' matched with sequenced pictures

story

'invent your own Romeo and Juliet' sequencing pictures and telling story from them

•*story*

pictures and 'key words' making posters for wall display using key words

TEXTS to be made available to pupils:

• standard school text
*abbreviated text
*prose version
*abbreviated prose text

(* Leon Garfield texts)
Animated Shakespeare films also useful

LOW COGNITIVE DEMAND

63

7 School systems

SCHOOL RESPONSIBILITIES

Clearly, the management and administration of a school has a key role to play in ensuring the greatest possible progress of all its pupils. It is sometimes said that the success or failure of a school stands or falls by the quality of its leadership and the effectiveness of the systems in place. They are the responsibility of senior management but are often delegated down to senior teachers or heads of department/faculty. Good systems will withstand staff change as they are not dependent on one charismatic individual. They need be realistic, practical and manageable, clearly understood, owned and used by all staff to be fully effective. These should form part of the whole school policy on assessment reporting and recording as it is the systems which put the parts of the policy into everyday practice.

Whatever separate procedures are used for the assessment of bilingual pupils or special needs pupils, they need to relate to National Curriculum criteria. OFSTED teams are asked to judge schools largely on the standards of achievement and the quality of teaching and learning. A recent survey which looked at educational support for minority ethnic communities reports that the most successful assessment practices "made effective use of comprehensive records to which all staff contributed, to raise the achievement of the pupils in National Curriculum terms". It concludes, "The best assessment recording and reporting procedures showed the pupil's attainment in National Curriculum terms and used the language stages to give a baseline from which to judge progress".(OFSTED 1994)

Special educational needs: Code of Practice

The Code of Practice (DFE 1994) on the identification and assessment of children with special educational needs gives guidance on the 'discharge of functions' under Part 111 of the 1993 Education Act for those pupils who fail to learn and progress within the general arrangements of the school. The Code recommends the general adoption of a staged model of which the first three stages are mainstream school based. At stages 4 and 5 the responsibility is shared with the LEA. The different stages are characterised thus:

- **STAGE 1**:
  class or subject teachers identify or register a child's special educational needs and, consulting the school's coordinator (SENco), take initial action

- **STAGE 2**:
  the SENco takes lead responsibility for gathering information and for coordinating the child's SEN provision, working with the child's teachers. An Individual Education Plan (IEP) is written and reviewed.

- **STAGE 3**:
  teachers and the SENco are supported by specialists from outside the school.

- **STAGE 4:**
  the LEA consider the need for statutory assessment and, if appropriate, make a multi-disciplinary assessment

- **STAGE 5:**
  the LEA consider the need for a statement of SEN and, if appropriate, make a statement and arrange, monitor and review provision

The demands and implications of the Code mean that the role of the school's coordinator for special educational needs (SENco) will have a key role in creating workable systems for the regular assessment, review and monitoring of those pupils registered. SENcos are also responsible for liaising with parents, agencies and support services. It is suggested that about 20 per cent of pupils may have special educational needs and that only about 2 per cent (nationally) are likely to have needs of sufficient severity to warrant statutory statements or special school places. As they will have considerable responsibility under the Code of Practice for monitoring at least 18 per cent of the pupils on role, it is to be hoped that SENcos are now given a status commensurate with other senior members of staff in recognition of the additional work and responsibility required.

BILINGUAL PUPILS REPRESENTATION ON THE CODE OF PRACTICE STAGES

In Chapter 1, I stated that schools should bear in mind the figures given above when checking the balance between bilingual pupils and those with special educational needs. As a rough guide the percentage of the bilingual pupil population should be reflected as a ratio of the school's registered SEN pupils. For example, take the case of a non selective secondary school of 1000 pupils which has a bilingual population of 40 per cent, i.e. 400 bilingual pupils. They could expect by law of averages to have a total of about 200 pupils registered across stages 1 to 5 of special educational need. Of these 200 they might expect 80 of these pupils (40 percent of the 200) to be bilingual.

This is a simple and fairly crude measurement but it will serve to inform you whether too great a proportion or too few of your bilingual pupils are perceived as having special educational needs. It is a way of checking your school's understanding that although the difficulties of language access of some bilingual children must not be confused with learning difficulties, some bilingual children (approximately 20 per cent) are equally likely to need to be registered as having special educational needs.

Of course there are all sorts of local variations on these 'national average' figures which serve only as a guide. In some schools and areas social conditions will create higher incidences of SEN than the national average. Bilingual children also come from a wide variety of backgrounds, but except in instances where research has proven that certain physical health/ sensory disabilities are more prevalent, there is nothing to suggest that children from ethnic minority communities should be either under or over represented in school populations as children with special educational need.

LEAS AND SEN AUDIT SYSTEMS

Many Local Educational Authorities are presently considering the introduction of a system of audit for special educational needs within their area. This is a funding issue and has arisen partly in response to Audit Commission reports on SEN and the rise in the numbers of pupils nationally who are being statemented. The statutory nature of these statements of SEN (roughly 2 per cent of all children) require considerable financial resourcing. This has meant that less and less money is available to the majority of pupils with SEN in schools without statements (18 per cent). Because of associated cuts in centrally provided services, it has been increasingly perceived by parents and teachers that statementing is the only way to ensure that extra resources will be available to meet a child's needs. Increasingly LEAs and schools are looking for a more equitable method of ensuring support in mainstream schools for pupils without recourse to statutory assessment.

Some authorities like Kent and Northhampton have devised and run a system of SEN audit which they have tested and revised in the light of experience. This devolves to schools the accountability for the identification of pupils prior to statementing and the responsibility for the interventions made. Other authorities are using these models on which to base their own. Central government argues that schools already have additional funding for factors in addition to APU (age-weighted pupil units) usually based on proxy indicators such as numbers of pupils entitled to free school meals and other socio-economic factors. The Code of Practice is therefore described as a 'nil resources' initiative! It is felt that with greater financial accountability and the delegation of budgets directly to schools, the significance of the publication of the Government's Code of Practice may well be a catalyst for further action. There is also a feeling in some quarters, that, because of central Government's close interest in systems of audit, they may be imposed on those LEAs who have not got their 'Acts' (sic!) together. Headteachers now have a considerable say in whether parts of the Education Budget are held for centrally organised services or delegated directly to schools. Therefore it is critical that there is agreement and moderation between schools so that funding for pupils at various stages of SEN registers is seen to be equitable and is used for the intended purpose. An audit system also means that schools and authorities are much more publicly accountable for expenditure on those children whom the money is intended to support.

Bilingual pupils presently represent over 60 per cent of the school population overall in Tower Hamlets. In a recent exercise in our Borough, a working group, which included headteachers, attempted to write descriptors of pupils at the school based stages of SEN as a proposal for an audit to be considered by local headteachers. Issues of support for bilingual pupils were directly addressed and written in. There are obviously dangers in doing this and it is an issue which has not been directly addressed elsewhere, probably because it is so contentious. The descriptors obviously fit local conditions and current levels of provision in Tower Hamlets. Although the feasibility of an audit is still being discussed and no decisions have been taken, the accompanying notes on bilingual pupils have been distributed to schools for their consideration in rewriting SEN policy documents where issues of concerning bilingual pupils must be addressed in operating the

Code of Practice proposals. The audit was written with descriptors fitting across the requirements of the Code to prevent a situation where two separate systems of assessing SEN pupils might be required from schools.

It is expected that local schools will have very clear guidelines for the expected progress in the acquisition of English at early language levels. If pupils continue to cause concern and there is clear evidence of their lack of progress after additional support and help with English has been given over a reasonable period of time and their progress with English closely monitored, then they may need to be identified and registered for SEN stage 1.

BILINGUAL PUPILS ON SEN REGISTERS
(notes for guidance)

STAGE 1 : ASSESSMENT

● It is expected that language support will continue and will contribute to a fuller picture of the bilingual child's acquisition of and learning in English

● Some assessment of first language will be helpful as this will help to clarify whether there is a delay or difficulty which is also apparent in the first language.

● Sight and hearing checks are particularly important at this stage to children learning in a second language, especially if the pupil is a recent arrival or refugee, as sensory loss cannot be assumed to have been identified at an earlier point

CURRICULAR NEEDS

● Even if pupils are registered for SEN, continued language support and assessment will be required. Pupils should still be targeted and included for group support with in the classroom.

● The additional help from the classteacher or other adult should include input from a language support teacher to suggest methodology, group activities, m a t e r i a l s and contextual referrants appropriate to support the child's learning in class. This support may also be given by the bilingual instructor/assistant for some of the time.

● Peer support in a group which includes other home language speakers is desirable but it is also important to ensure that the group includes more fluent English speaking peers.

EQUIPMENT/MATERIALS

● Bilingual pupils may require increased access to shared equipment and differentiated materials including bilingual or translated texts.

ACCESS TO AGENCIES

● Pupils may need access to local resources of advice/support in the community. If school staff or home and community contacts cannot be provided in a minority language then translation/interpretation services may become appropriate.

NB *Schools may need advice and /or INSET on the early identification of bilingual pupils with SEN*

STAGE 2 : ASSESSMENT*(as for Stage 1 plus -:)*

● A first language assessment of expressive/receptive language would give valuable further information. Some assessment of conceptual development through first language would also provide significant additional evidence.

CURRICULAR NEEDS

● In addition to the language support provided in class, targeted and specific language support may be appropriate for some bilingual pupils at stage 2.

● Support to address specific curricular objectives could be provided by a language support teacher or bilingual instructor. This must then be clearly specified on the Individual Education Plan and should be additional to any other targeted curriculum support provided for learning or other difficulties.

ACCESS TO AGENCIES

● Advice from bilingual SEN staff may be appropriate at this stage. A bilingual speech and language assessment may also be appropriate.

STAGE 3 : ASSESSMENT *(as for Stages 1 & 2 plus -:)*

● The bilingual SEN advisory teacher may be involved in assessing difficulties or in contributing to an IEP at this stage.

● This may involve the expertise in assessment skills from a member of staff. This could be done by a monolingual teacher with these skills working alongside a bilingual member of staff with an understanding of SEN.

ACCESS TO AGENCIES

● Use of the Bengali Parent Advisors (a local service currently provided from GEST funding) may be advisable at this stage

8 Conclusions

It is to be hoped that the wide range of ideas and descriptions of various aspects of assessment in this book help individuals and schools see more clearly that although language and learning difficulties should not be confused, some bilingual pupils are likely to have special educational needs. Teachers need to trust and rely on their own professional skills and abilities to assess the competence of bilingual pupils in collaboration with colleagues. Schools need to establish good policies and reliable systems for recording and reporting to ensure that pupils are neither overlooked nor wrongly assigned.

The key to accurate and well considered assessment decisions about children whose learning is causing concern is the quality of the consideration in the search for information and evidence. The solutions are often to be found within the mainstream mixed ability classroom where the education of bilingual pupils and those who may have special educational needs is a part every teacher's job. The assessment of pupils' needs is increasingly likely to rely on their observation and evidence rather than on a formal testing of cognitive processing alone. Equally there is less likelihood that factors will be seen as deficits within the child, separate somehow, from an evaluation of the adequacy and appropriateness of classroom methodology and materials. In the same way as language and learning are inextricably linked ,so there is an undoubted relationship between self esteem, behaviour and learning.

That the good classroom practice of skilled and experienced teachers can support the learning and achievement of bilingual pupils in school is in abundant evidence in many schools. Hopefully the ideas developed in this book will renew your faith in your own skills and good practice and encourage you and your colleagues to develop this important aspect of your work.

Useful Addresses

- **The Collaborative Learning Project** is run by Stuart Scott as a 'swapshop' for teachers materials developed from collaborative and group work in classrooms. To join you send in your materials. A catalogue of materials for sale at photocopied rates is available. Stuart is available to run workshops on using/developing collaborative games and activities in the classroom and is also doing a lot of work with European countries (also see Intercultural Exchange Programme below).

  Stuart Scott
  17 Barford St. London N1 OQB
  Tel. 0171 226 8885

- **The Intercultural Exchange Programme** is supported by the Commission of the European Union and the United Kingdom Departments for Education. It offers various projects as a forum for issues of common interest with European counterparts in the teaching of bilingual/ethnic minority children. Up to date Information can be gleaned from :

  Mandy Slattery
  17 Barford St, London NI OQB
  Tel. 0171 226 8885

- **NALDIC** (National Association of Language Development in the Curriculum) is a recently formed network for UK teachers "working for pupils with English as an additional language". For membership and information about local networks, contact:

  Cressida Jupp
  c/o NALDIC, Hounslow Language Service, Hounslow Education Centre, Martindale Road, Hounslow TW4 7 HE
  Tel: (via Education Services) 0181 862 5352

- **NASEN** (National Association for Special Educational Needs) publishes two excellent journals with articles on various aspects of SEN: Support for Learning and the British Journal of Special Education. It also provides a national forum for discussion and debate through local associations and sponsors Special Needs Education Exhibitions and Seminars.

  Membership queries: York House, Exhall Grange, Wheelwright Lane, Coventry CV7 9HP
  Tel: 01203 362414

  Journals and Publications: NASEN enterprises, 2 Lichfield Road, Stafford. ST17 4JX
  Tel: 01785 46872

- **Tower Hamlets Language Support Service** distributes the books marked ** in the references. A catalogue is also available of materials such as tapes, story props and packs. Packs for the teaching of Bengali as a modern foreign language at GCSE are also available.

Tower Hamlets Language Support Service
Professional Development Centre, English St. London E3 4TA
Tel: 0181 981 0183

- **The ESL/SEN Network** at SENJIT is a useful forum for teachers in the Greater London area which organises termly talks/workshops on various areas of interest. Information and contacts via:

Nick Peacey
SENJIT Institute of Education
University of London
20 Bedford Way, London WC1H OAL
Tel: 0171 612 6273

References & Further Reading

Ayers,H; Clarke, D; Ross,A & Bonathan, M. (1993)
Assessing Individual Needs.
David Fulton. London

Barrs, M; Ellis,S; Hester,H. & Kelly, A.V. (1988)
The Primary Language Record Handbook. C.L.P.E. London

Barrs,M; Ellis, S; Hester,H . & Thomas, A. (1990)
Patterns of Learning C.L.P.E. London

Barthorpe,T. & Visser, J. (1989)
Differentiation: Your Responsibility.
NASEN Stafford

Bennett,N & Barnes,D. (1992)
Managing Classroom Groups.
Simon &Schuster

Bourne, J. & McPake, J.(1991)
Partnership Teaching.
NFER/DES for HMSO London

Buxton, C. (1994)
Language Activities for Bilingual Learners.
Tower Hamlets Language Support Service. London **

Cinamon, D. & Gravelle, M.(1988)
Bilingualism is NOT a learning difficulty. Gnosis 12.
LDA Wisbech

Clay, M. (1979)
The Early Detection of Reading Difficulties.
Heinemann. London

Cline,T & Frederickson, N. (1991)
Bilingual Pupils and the National Curriculum:
Overcoming difficulties in Teaching and Learning.
University College London

Cline, T. & Frederickson, N. (1994)
Progress in Curriculum Related Assessment for Bilingual Pupils.
Multilingual Matters. Avon

C.R.E. (1986)
The Teaching of English as a Second Language:
The Report of a Formal Enquiry in Calderdale LEA.
Commission for Racial Equality. London

Cummins, J. (1984)
Bilingualism and Special Education: Issues in Assessment and Pedagogy.
Multilingual Matters. Avon

Desforges,M. & Kerr, T. (1984)
Developing bilingual children's English in school.
Educational and Child Psychology Vol.1 No 1

D.E.S. (1985)
Education for All:
The Report of the Committee of Enquiry into the Education of Children from Ethnic
Minorities. (the Swann Report)
H.M.S.O. London

D.F.E. (1994)
**Code of Practice on the Identification and Assessment of Special Educational
Needs.**
Department for Education. London

Dulay, H & Burt, M. (1974)
Natural sequences in second language acquisition.
Language Learning 24

Dulay, H; Burt, M. & Krashen,S. (1982)
Language Two.
Oxford University Press.

Duncan,D.(ed) (1989)
Working with Bilingual Language Disability.
Chapman & Hall. London and New York

Field, C. (1992)
Collaborative Learning Project: Romeo and Juliet.
Tower Hamlets Language Support Service. London **

Graf, V. (1992)
Minimising the Inappropriate Referral and Placement of Ethnic Minority Students in
Special Education in Cline, T. (ed)
The Assessment of Special Educational Needs: International Perspectives.
Routledge. London

Hall, D. (1994)
Differentiating the Secondary Curriculum in Cline, T. & Frederickson, N. (eds)
Progress in Curriculum Related Assessment for Bilingual Pupils.
Multilingual Matters. Avon

Kerr, T & Desforges, M. (1988)
Developing Bilingual Children's English in School in Verma, G. & Pumfrey,P. (eds)
Educational Attainments: Issues and Outcomes in Multicultural Education.
Falmer Press. London

Krashen,S. (1981) **Second Language Acquisition and Second Language Learning.**
Pergamon Press. Oxford

Mattes, L. & Omark, D. (1984)
Speech and Language Assessment for the Bilingual Handicapped.
College Hill Press. San Diego. California

Miller, N. (ed) (1984)
Bilingualism and Language Disability: Assessment and Remediation.
College Hill Press. San Diego. California

National Oracy Project (1993) Baddeley,G. (ed)
Learning Together Through Talk KS1 & 2 and Kemeny, H. (ed)
Learning Together Through Talk KS3 &4
Hodder & Stoughton

OFSTED (1993)
Handbook for the Inspection of Schools. H.M.S.O. London

OFSTED (1994)
Educational Support for Minority Ethnic Communities:
A survey of educational provision funded under Section 11 of the 1966 Local
Government Act. Ofsted Publications Centre. London

Reid,J; Forrestal,P & Cook,J (1989)
Small Group Learning in the Classroom
Chalk Face Press

Robson, A. (1986)
Bilingual learners- school based assessment. Gnosis 10.
LDA Wisbech

Robson.A. (1991)
Differentiation for Bilingual Pupils in the National Curriculum in Cline,T &
Frederickson, N.
Bilingual Pupils and the National Curriculum.
University College London

Shah, S. (1990) **Assessment by monolingual teachers of developing bilinguals at Key Stage 1** Multicultural Teaching Vol. 9 No. 1

Shell, R. (1992) **Language Works.**
Tower Hamlets Learning by Design Block C. the PDC, English Street, London E3 4TA
Tel. 0181 983 1944 Fax 0181 983 1932

Skutnabb- Kangas, T. (1981)
Bilingualism or Not.
Multilingual Matters. Avon

Thomlinson, S. (1982)
A Sociology of Special Education.
Routledge Kegan Paul. London

Visser, J. (1993)
Differentiation: Making it work. NASEN Stafford

Wright, A. (1991) The Assessment of Bilingual Pupils with Reported Learning
Difficulties in Cline,T & Frederickson, N.
Bilingual Pupils and the National Curriculum.
University College London

** Publications thus marked are available from
Tower Hamlets Language Support Service (see Useful Addresses)

IDENTIFICATION AND ASSESSMENT
Bilingual Learners

■ **BASIC INFORMATION**
About the Child at Home and in the Community

■ **SCREENING**
Physical/Medical/Sensory

■ **HYPOTHESIS THEORY**
Consider & Disregard

Asking Questions
Chapter 4

? Learning Successfully ?

?

?

Chapter 5
Collecting Evidence

Chapter 6
Planning Support

■ **LANGUAGE LEVEL**
Stages of English.
Section 11 Files and Records

■ **INDIVIDUAL ACTION PLAN**

■ **FIRST LANGUAGE DEVELOPMENT**
Information ?

■ **DIFFERENTIATION**

■ **CURRICULUM RELATED ASSESSMENT**
(**Cummins Matrix**)
Curriculum Planning.

■ **READING STRATEGIES**
Scales/Recovery/'THRIVE'

■ **SAMPLES OF WORK**
Pupil self assessment
School records/assessments AR&R

■ **SCHOOLS SYSTEM OF SUPPORT** (Chapter 7)

■ **NATIONAL CURRICULUM ATTAINMENT**

BILINGUAL CHILDREN
WHAT THE RESEARCH
TELLS US

- Children take up to two years to develop 'basic interpersonal communication skills' (playground/street survival language) BUT it takes from five to seven years to acquire the full range of literacy skills ('cognitive academic language proficiency') needed to cope with the literacy demands of GCSE.

- A silent (receptive) period is natural the learning of a second language and not a sign of learning difficulties in the first/early stages.

- There are developmental factors in common to both native and second language acquisition. Pupils learn roughly the same regardless of their first language background.

- Teachers /schools should have basic information available about the language backgrounds of bilingual pupils. (see Chapter 4)

- There should be an awareness by all that a focus on mother tongue is a valuable channel to support learning and NOT a hindrance. Teachers should not advocate the use of English only, either at school or at home.

- Parents should be encouraged to share language and literacy in speaking and listening as well as in reading and writing. This can be as valuable in first/home language as in English.

- Bilingualism can be educationally enriching and has a positive effect on intellectual performance.

- Bilingualism should be valued as a special achievement.

- Where there are academic difficulties, teachers should first critically examine the teaching they are offering in terms of motivation and the language used.

The Bilingual Pupil at Home and in the Community

Basic Family Details

Full Name .... D.O.B. ....

Name child is called at home .... Age Now ....

Name to be called at school (if different) ....

Arrival date in UK (if not British born) ....

Length of previous schooling abroad ....

Names of schools/LEAs in UK ....

Number of terms of UK schooling ....

Date of long extended absences from schooling ....

Place of birth .... Religion ....

Does child live with both parents as part of family unit? .... Festivals observed ....

If not who are carers? ....

Mothers name .... Dietary needs ....

Fathers name ....

(School correspondence should be addressed to ....

Most useful written language for family is ....

Names and ages of siblings ....

....

....

Languages

Languages spoken at home by pupil to   Mother .... Grandparents ....

                                         Father .... Siblings ....

Languages used by family members to child

Can child read/write languages other than English?   write .... read ....

Is child learning to read/write in languages other than English? ....

Community Links

Does child attend any school/class in community/..

Mother tongue class .... community school .... religious .... Mosque/classes ....

What languages are used taught there? ....

What is the name/address of organisation? ....

....

....

Who is contact person for group? ....

Is interpreter needed for teacher to communicate with parents ? ....

If so, who might this be? ....

Family view of important illnesses/or other medical factors seen as important ....

Is child right handed? left handed?................... Should child be using glasses hearing aid/other aids for learning? ....

....

Does child require any regular medication during school day ....

Secondary pupil languages form

What languages do I use?

What languages do they use to me?

Mother

Father

Sisters & Brothers

Grandparents

languages used by ....

I think that I talk ....a bit   quite well   very well

I read ....a bit   quite well   very well

I can copy ....

I write it   a bit   quite well   very well

When I think about home, I think in ....

When I am at school, I think in ....

Can I say all I want to in ....?   Yes   No

Can I say all I want to in English? .... Yes   No

I think I am best at using the .... Language, at present

Date completed ....

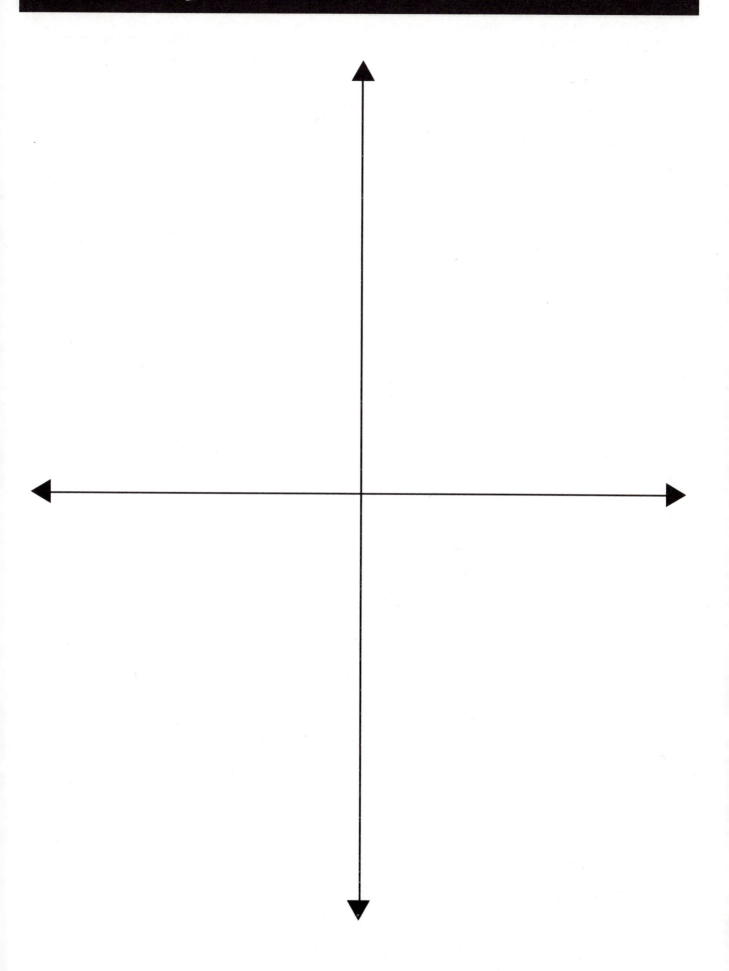